THE PIRATE PICTURE

THE
PIRATE PICTURE

by
Rayner Thrower

BARNES
&NOBLE
BOOKS
NEW YORK

This edition published by Barnes & Noble, Inc.,
by arrangement with Phillimore & Co., Ltd.

1993 Barnes & Noble Books

ISBN 1-56619-148-3

Printed and bound in the United States of America
M 9 8 7 6 5 4 3 2 1

CONTENTS

CONTENTS

PREFACE

It is doubtful whether a complete history of piracy can be written so long after the days when it started to become a plague on all maritime activities. Pirates themselves were hardly likely to record their deeds, and this explains, to some extent, why writers of certain books and novels have often drawn on their imagination about much that went on, and have even romanticised a group of men who were simply rogues of the sea.

While much surviving factual information concerns the Caribbean and Indian Oceans, these were only important regions for two centuries, whereas pirates have menaced shipping everywhere for thousands of years. Fortunately, the classical writers have given us a limited amount of information about happenings in the ancient world and the pattern of some of these events, revealed by recent archaeological research, shows how piracy fitted into the changing character of world trade. So to make this past situation clearer, the main features of world trade in bygone days have been presented briefly in this book; much more could be written about this, but would be out of place in a book of this character.

Coming to what may be regarded as more recent times, some of the facts presented which may not be generally known, were accidentally discovered during the years I was preparing my book, describing conditions in the early sailing ships (*Life at Sea in the Age of Sail*). This led me to seek additional information about some of the robberies and pillages forming such a feature of maritime life, as deep sea trade developed in European, New World, and, later, Far Eastern waters.

Much of the story herein has been made possible by the generous help of various librarians providing facts tucked away in rare tracts and volumes. In particular I should mention Mr. Payne, Librarian at the Royal College of Physicians, for access to the treasures in the general collection at the College, the Librarians of the British Library and in the Library of the Commonwealth and Dominions Office; while my neighbour, Mr. John Parker has allowed me unrestricted access to his remarkable collection of books about early navigation. For much of the present knowledge about the remote contacts of the Egyptians and the Levantine mariners with Southern Africa I am indebted to the Librarian of the State Library in Pretoria.

One problem has been to find contemporary illustrations, so scarce, to enliven the text. Some of these have come from my own collection, but the British Library has provided Plates 1 and 10; the Curator of the Armouries, Tower of London, Plates 4 and 11; Harveys of Bristol, Plate 8; Montagu Motor Museum, Plate 9; and the National Maritime Museum, London, Plate 12.

In deciding how far it was desirable to incorporate material which might be regarded as controversial and, at times, even conflicting with current opinion, I have been guided throughout by what Certuis, the Roman, wrote over two thousand years ago. 'I neither dare to affirm positively what I doubt of, nor can I think it proper to omit what I have been told'.

Captain Frank Dibble, Master Mariner, kindly read the manuscript to ensure its technical accuracy.

CHAPTER I

PIRATES AND PRIVATEERS

JUST AS the Mediterranean and its shores was the cradle of so much affecting mankind, so it was the place where we first heard about piracy. This started thousands of years ago and steadily increased with the growing prosperity and trade of that region.

Over the ages the pattern of piracy in different parts of the world has shown considerable variation, not only because of the changes in the trades which provided the prizes, but also in the different sorts of people involved and the arms available to them. For instance, in Northern Europe, Norsemen armed with swords and spears set the pattern there with their fearsome raids into the North Sea and adjacent waters. Later, in the Caribbean, it was high-lighted by the early buccaneers, mostly of French origin, armed with knives and pistols. Finally, in the Indian Ocean came the time when there were ships roaming about some-times prepared to fight their opponents with naval guns.

Piracy always seems to have been regarded as one of the means of livelihood offered by the sea. Thucydides (471 B.C.), that remarkable Greek historian, writing about conditions in the Mediterranean long before his time, says how many inhabitants of its islands and of the littoral in the eastern end turned to piracy for their own gain and to maintenance for the needy, making most of their livelihood by this means; an employment not bringing disgrace but, rather, glory.[1] Aristotle (384 B.C.), too, showed how piracy and brigandage were regarded as a form or production as other men support themselves by hunting or fishing.[2] Throughout maritime history it has gone on in nearly every

1

place where ships sailed. While it may be easy to criticise these scourges of humanity there is no doubt that what some of these men, and even women, achieved, often in the face of overwhelming odds, boggles the imagination. It is disappointing that authentic accounts of much that happened are so scarce; but, after all, why should there be many available? Few involved could read or write anyway, and there were no Sunday newspapers ready to pay large sums for a ghosted story. Indeed, few robbers, and pirates were robbers, are ever likely to be very ready to reveal much about their methods and exploits to the general public. Gripping stories have always been favourite inventions by novelists and writers of boys' books, but with what is actually known about pirates and their doings there is no need to draw very much on imagination for thrills.

Although it may be a distinction without much difference, robbery at sea, as compared with robbery ashore, has always been associated with violence and killing. In fact, this is precisely what has made it so odious. However, over the years other acts besides blatant sea robbery have been declared by statute to constitute piracy. Thus any shipmaster or other seafarer who betrayed his trust, or made off with any ship or goods, or who voluntarily yielded these up to pirates, came to be regarded as a pirate himself; also, in the course of time, anyone trading with known pirates or aiding them committed an offence. Just as the Romans in their day regarded it, so piracy ultimately came to be considered an offence against mankind as a whole rather than against any particular state or individual. This concept finally resulted in making it punishable in the courts of any country to which alleged offenders might be taken.

While for centuries the practice was widespread around the British Isles, it was not until as late as the time of William III (1688-1702) that English law, covering its various aspects, was finally tightened up and enforced whenever possible. Such legislation was not popular among many ordinary folk ashore who welcomed the stolen cargoes of merchandise which eventually reached the open market to be sold cheaply; indeed, housewives actually complained if such cargoes had not been on sale for some time, very much as people did in later days when smugglers were busy.

Whatever the niceties of their legal position may have been there is no doubt that from Tudor times well into the 17th century the activities of pirates materially influenced the course of world events. A striking example is that there would probably be no Holland as we know it today, but for Dutch pirates in 1572 who directed their energies to driving Spanish invaders from occupation of their homeland; a strange event concerning which details will be given later. Then again, long ago, as described in the next chapter, the Mediterranean piracy which was rampant for around two thousand years B.C. exerted equally remarkable effects on occasions, not simply on the trade but even on the population distribution of that region.

Corsair, a word derived from the Italian *corsare* or *corso,* implying courses or excursions, was specially applied to the Barbary pirates who went into business in the beginning of the 14th century at the western end of the Mediterranean as one result of the Christian conquest of Spain from the Moors. After this conquest the Moslem Andalusians (the Moors) and the Moslem seamen, later called corsairs, were expelled from Spain after occupying that country for 500 years. It was in revenge against the increasing Christian domination of the Mediterranean that many Moorish seamen turned to piracy, which became a very profitable occupation at a time when the greater part of the world maritime trade was concentrated there. Their activities were highly organised, so much so that along the Moslem North African coast they had regular receivers of stolen goods which were sold on commission. Any important passengers captured were held to ransom and the others sold into slavery. The corsair menace to sea trade lasted for several centuries, and eventually became so serious that even various governments in Northern Europe were prepared to make deals with corsairs in attempts to protect their shipping. Despite such deals they remained a scourge until 1700, when their activities were curtailed by an English Admiral, Sir John Narborough. Despite the activities of Narborough along the Barbary

Coast, some thirty years later, in 1731, the French Mediterranean fleet under Rear-Admiral Duguay Trouin (a rank
this one-time privateer captain ultimately attained) was
ordered to make the Beys of Algeria and of Tunis keep their
piratical subjects under control, because they had again
become such a menace to peaceful traders. French merchantmen had always suffered as much as any from Barbary
pirates, and long after the death of the celebrated Cardinal
Richelieu in 1642, despite the decline in French maritime
power otherwise, ships originally built at his instigation
for the navy were kept in commission in an attempt to
prevent corsair activity. The corsairs were not finally
suppressed until about 1830 when British men-of-war, freed
from pre-occupation with the Napoleonic wars, were able
to take the further necessary action. Here, again, the French
were involved, because at that time they were trying to
establish themselves in Algeria, where they concluded a
treaty with the neighbouring Bey in Tunisia. This Bey was
particularly addicted to piracy, and in part of the treaty
was an undertaking to give up his habit.

The word 'buccaneer' and 'pirate' are always associated,
but for a long time there was a distinct difference between
the true meanings of the words. Originally, buccaneers were
French colonists in Hispaniola and on Tortuga, an island
off its north coast, who made their living by hunting wild
cattle and pigs. The flesh was fried in a special manner to
make buccan, thereby providing a local supply of preserved
meat used both by the inhabitants of the West Indies and by
ships requiring to replenish their stores. From this word
buccan, applied to dried meat, came the term buccaneer,
simply to describe men who made it.

The real origin of the word buccan is nothing less than
macabre. As is well known the original inhabitants of the
West Indian islands were all cannibals. The Spanish word
for cannibal is *caribal,* hence Caribs to designate these
original islanders. At a cannibal feast human flesh was cooked
on a sort of outdoor grid-iron or grill called a *bucan* (Plate 1).[1]
It appears that some of the human meat was preserved by
the Caribs for future consumption, very much in the manner

that buccaning of beef and pork was done later on by the Europeans in Hispaniola, who must have learnt the method from the Caribs. In his voyages, Hakluyt, when writing about the Caribs, refers to flesh 'dressed in the smoke which in their language they called boucaned'. In course of time the Spanish so harried the French buccaneers they were compelled to abandon their peaceful way of life ashore and to take to the sea as pirates. The term buccaneer is freely used, somewhat incorrectly, to designate all the ruffians who left their mark on the history of Central America and the New England coast, the name given to the Atlantic seaboard of the English colonies in North America.

Freebooter is a word almost synonymous with the word buccaneer, after this had lost its original meaning and had become just another term for pirate. According to Captain Burney, writing in 1816, the word freebooter was used long before the days of Tortuga to describe men cruising about seeking unlawful gain. The word finally came to be used to describe the French filibusters from Hispaniola who became sea-rovers: men, originally buccaneers, who gave up hunting to go to sea for free play or free booty. It has been suggested that freebooter was a corruption of the Dutch *vribuiter* because words from all the European languages were so thoroughly mixed up by seamen of these days as to comprise practically a language of its own.

Privateers were originally quite respectable, but gradually fell from grace. What happened was that wealthy men fitted out ships at their own expense to constitute privately-owned men-of-war, fighting on behalf of their country of origin on the high seas and not in what would now be called territorial waters. The rewards for doing this were substantial, because, after one-fifth of the value of any enemy ship captured had been taken by the Crown, the balance went to the privateer owner and crew. During our wars in the 18th century privateers were given an additional inducement by getting £10 for every gun in any French ship captured. Apart from the code of rules governing the division of spoils, the captain, like the captain of a naval ship, was permitted to flog any sailor for indiscipline or dangerous offences such as smoking a pipe without a lid or having a naked candle below deck. These offences were regarded very seriously in days when a fire in any ship often led to her total destruction and the death of those on board. There were no lifeboats or air-sea rescue services. Rules to lessen the ever-present fire risk were enforced equally strictly even in pirate vessels: in ordinary merchantmen flogging was not permitted, and the usual penalty was stoppage of pay, an effective punishment for any man when, unlike today, money was hard to come by.

We first hear about privateers at the time of the French wars in the early 16th century when these ships were usually privately owned; sometimes syndicates were formed to commission them, and one such syndicate, formed by the publicans in Chester, is described by Froude.[4] At one time or another privateers were fitted out in many of the principal English ports. Liverpool provided most of them in the 18th century, when they were widely used to augment naval strength. The most celebrated English privateer captain was a Liverpool man, Fortunatus Wright, who for some few years was the scourge of the French in the Mediterranean; in one year alone (1746) he captured 16 of their ships. After many more successes he was lost at sea in a storm off Sicily. Most European nations operated privateers, but the French ships were always respected because of the efficient way they were fitted out and handled.

The last days of the privateer were during the war of 1812 between Great Britain and the United States of America, when well-found American privateers made their presence really felt against British shipping, even as far as European waters. Incidentally, they were responsible for sinking some of the Algerian corsairs who had re-established themselves to some extent after the original attack on them by Narborough and Duguay Trouin more than a hundred years earlier.

Over the centuries the position and status of privateers was, in practice, usually obscure, a situation made worse by the fact that when some war in which they had engaged ended they often became pirates. One man, who should have known better, was Prince Rupert of the Rhine. In 1648 he set himself up as a privateer and operated genuinely enough to start with, but then decided to turn pirate and went to the West Indies. There his activities were ended by being wrecked off the Virgin Islands in 1653. From this disaster he escaped, and somehow returned to France where he lived for some time before finally moving to London, dying there in 1682.

One of the more extraordinary privateer stories concerns a ship in the West Indies, during the French wars around 1800, actually commissioned by no less a person than Admiral Sir Hyde Parker while serving there. She was commanded by a man named Antonine, who soon got into disfavour locally by behaving more or less as a pirate; from Antonine's depredations the real owner benefited. Since this so-called privateer was owned by an admiral, the only way of dealing with such a bizarre situation was by private enterprise. Aggrieved men in Jamaica clubbed together to fit out a ship of their own to catch the raider, and this was successfully done. Antonine was duly tried as a pirate and sentenced to be hanged, but the sentence was not carried out because he was poisoned by his wife while in prison awaiting execution.

During the time from 1661–1683, when the great Colbert was laying the foundations for a proper French navy, much in the same way as Samuel Pepys was then doing for England, he encouraged privateers while naval strength was being built up. As an additional inducement to French privateer crews, apart from prize money, there was a bonus system which permitted them to pillage for the space of one hour any ship which had proved difficult to capture.

It was Colbert who introduced Letters of Marque for privateers, a kind of licensing system soon adopted by other countries to regularise privateer activities internationally. But the system must have been carelessly applied. There is the oft-told story about one out-and-out pirate operating in the Caribbean in the 17th century, who started sailing as a privateer under a supposed Letter of Marque he had purchased from the Governor of a Danish West Indian island. It was written in Danish and, when translated, merely entitled the holder to hunt for goats and pigs in Hispaniola. Further attempts were made by various European governments to improve the licensing of privateers, and in these attempts Colbert again took the lead by requiring from privateers what the French termed caution money. This money, depending on the size of the vessel, could amount to as much as £5,000 and was held by the Government to ensure good behaviour. Later, in the reign of William III, the English and Dutch Governments followed suit and required privateer owners to deposit a bond; £1,500 if the ship did not exceed 150 tons burden, and £3,000 if larger. When claims were made for damages suffered through some allegedly unlawful act by a privateer, the aggrieved party was compensated by money from the bond, and failure to pay compensation rendered a privateer liable to forfeiture of a commission. How often such bonds were actually deposited and whether successful claims on them were made is uncertain. Letters of Marque were finally abolished by the Congress of Paris in 1856, but this treaty was not ratified by the U.S.A.; so, if it wished, the American Government could still license privateers!

On the whole English privateers were not as successful as the Frenchmen; English men-of-war were the ships mainly instrumental in destroying French merchant shipping. But there were not so many French merchantmen as English merchantmen to be taken, so English ships suffered terrible losses: in one year, 1689, 420 English and Dutch vessels were captured by French privateers. In the total of 40 years we were at war with France, between 1656 and 1783, 4,344 prizes were actually sold in Dunkirk alone; of these 251 were in the single year of 1751. The French have much justification for still honouring the memory of such privateer captains as Jean Bart, Duguay Trouin and Laville, who featured so largely in their early maritime history fully described by C. B. Norman.[5] When we finally captured the French bases freely scattered throughout the world, these serious attacks on English shipping ceased.

Nelson in his day said that privateers were no better than pirates, but a hundred years before Nelson there was a New England clergyman in Boston who said this and more. His name was Cotton Mather, and he used to take pleasure in periodically preaching what were called his hanging sermons. Pirates caught off the New England coast were nearly always hanged, and quite a number would be executed in batches at the same time, hence these sermons to them. In one of the homilies he is quoted as saying that 'the privateering stroke so easily degenerated into the Piratical and the Privateering Trade is usually carried on with an Unchristian Temper and proves an inlet into so much Debauchery and Iniquity'.

In England the hanging of pirates was done without ceremony; any convicted at the Old Bailey were simply hanged on the Thames foreshore nearby, between high and low water watermarks, as a warning to others. A nicety in the technique was that the victims' toes just touched the water. Protests from the citizens of London ultimately resulted in a less obtrusive site further down river being used for exhibition purposes.

Such as it was, the New Englanders showed more concern for the spiritual welfare of condemned men than was the case in England. By Acts of Parliament passed in the reigns of both William III and George I, participants in any form of piracy were, on conviction, excluded from the benefits of clergy. The William III Act was rather more charitable in other respects. A section provided that, if during the defence of a merchantman against attack, any seaman was killed, his widow was entitled to a bounty, the amount being determined by the value of the cargo in his ship. Wounded seamen likewise were entitled to a bounty and, if disabled, were eligible for admission to Greenwich Hospital which no seaman could enter unless he had served in the Navy.

As overseas trade was developed by European countries the risk of attacks on merchant ships, even if they were armed, was considerably reduced by the convoy system originally devised by the Spaniards in the 16th century specially for their homeward-bound treasure ships. By engaging such a convoy Sir Richard Grenville was lost in *Revenge*. The only hope of success against a convoy was to attack a straggler. A particular English form of defence against attack on merchantmen was the development of charters of merchantmen. This was a system which differed from an ordinary convoy inasmuch as all the shipowners concerned paid a sum of money into a common pool. The sum paid depended upon the tonnage of the ship, and from the pool were made good any losses due to attack during the voyage. These charters were well managed, with a senior captain appointed as admiral, supported by a vice-admiral and a rear-admiral. The charter system was the beginning of marine insurance as we know it today, covering damage or loss to hulls or cargoes. This gradually became a business on its own in 1688, operating from Lloyd's coffee house in London. Odd lone merchantmen in dangerous waters often joined up with a convoy for a while to obtain some protection.

When pirates or privateers were reported to be active near the course of a lone merchantman many a captain must have looked to any defences his ship possessed and how these could be strengthened. An example of how such precautions could go wrong was provided by a Liverpool ship, *Thomas,* in 1797 on passage from the Guinea Coast to Barbados. The master, Captain M'Quay, instructed many of the slaves on board in the use of firearms against possible attacks by French privateers known to be about. The outcome of this was that the armed negroes seized the ship, and the captain with 12 of his crew just managed to escape in a ship's boat. Somehow their navigation was at fault, and only after 38 days the boat drifted ashore in Barbados with three survivors, two men and a boy. This boat voyage provides one of the authentic instances of cannibalism known to have occurred under similar circumstances. As was written in a letter about the event:

> And you might see
> The longings of the animal arise
> (Although they spoke not) in
> their wolfish eyes.

What actually happened was that lots were cast to select the victim, who asked that he might be bled to death by the ship's surgeon, who was in the party and possessed his instruments. When a suitable vein was cut some men had a drink of blood, while the others refrained until the body was jointed up and shared out between all except the two men and the boy who survived. All the others went mad and gradually died off, but there is no explanation given why this happened. Unfortunately the boy, completely exhausted, was drowned as the survivors finally got ashore.[6]

Some East Indiamen carried soldiers, but from the lists I have examined it is impossible to determine whether they were passengers travelling to or from the Far East armed forces of the English East India Company, or whether they were on board to help defend the ship against possible attacks. Only for the first few years after the incorporation did the East India Company own ships used for its eastern trade. Thereafter until the end of the 18th century all ships were chartered, but such close control was exercised over everything concerning them that, for practical purposes, they might have been Company property. On one occasion, when an East Indiaman was actually boarded by pirates, some soldiers were unable to contribute much to the defence of the ship, owing to lack of training in how to meet the special kind of hand-to-hand fighting in which their opponents were so skilled. That regular soldiers could show up so badly in fighting of this nature aroused much criticism at the time.

Notes

1. Thucydides I, 5.
2. Aristotle, Politics I. 1256 (Jowett edn. 1881).
3. *The Black Democracy*. H. P. Davis (Allen and Unwin).
4. *English Seamen in the Sixteenth Century*. 1895.
5. *The French Corsairs*. Norman, C. B., 1880.
6. *Letters from the Virgin Islands*. The Rev. R. C. Thomas, London, 1843.

CHAPTER II

ANCIENT PIRACY

A GLANCE AT THE MAP makes it possible to obtain a good understanding of the reasons throughout history which made piracy so easy and profitable to the many communities established around the Mediterranean. The very nature of the geography, with hundreds of islands and an indented coastline, made sea transport a necessity; further, attacks on ships mostly by gangs based ashore were easy in the days when most ships did not sail out of sight of land and often anchored inshore by night. Reliance on sea transport was emphasised by the difficulty and, in certain places, the impossibility of establishing land communications owing to the rough and often mountainous nature of the Mediterranean hinterland. In these rough territories bandits flourished; so travellers had to face either bandits ashore or pirates afloat. The very word pirate is derived from the ancient Greek word *peirates*.

This chapter is not intended to be the story of ancient navigations, but some of these were so directly connected with the contemporary pirate picture that an understanding of them provides a background to the conditions then existing, and the temptations for the unscrupulous. At this distance in time it is obvious that important details about many things that went on are lost. Indeed, there is even disagreement among scholars just how to interpret correctly any informative details that do exist.

Homer, writing as early as 850 B.C., indicates that piracy had always been an evil; and how Minos, one of the Cretan kings, in 2000 B.C., did much to keep it in check. After the days of Minos, Crete was occupied by the people later known as the Phoenicians. The Levantine mariners who had various bases in the Eastern Mediterranean are often spoken of as Phoenicians, but not until the time of Homer is the word Pheonikes first applied to the people of the coastal strip of Asia Minor, later called Syrophenicia, of which Tyre and Sidon were the principal ports. These people came to dominate world maritime trade; indeed, the commercial instincts of the Levantines seem to have been as well developed three or four thousand years ago as they are today. During Odysseus' wanderings (described in the *Odyssey*) he met a Phoenician 'practised in deceit, a greedy knave . . .'. The use of the term 'merchant prince' was first applied to some of the inhabitants of Tyre and Sidon. Their colonisation of various parts of the Western Mediterranean was a fairly late development in expansion from the Levant, and lasted until the Roman western conquests in 300 B.C. How quite fantastic Phoenician wealth and power must have been is fully set out in Ezekiel 26, 27 (*c.* 600 B.C.); the pity of it is that we do not know the precise situation of many of the places mentioned by the prophet. Such information that has survived chiefly covers the later centuries of their prowess.

Long before Tyre and Sidon became so celebrated, the nearby city of Byblos (modern Gebeil) was a maritime centre during the heyday of the Pharaohs. Adjacent ports were equally busy and more or less under Egyptian direction, partly because the Egyptians possessed no ocean-going ships of their own, a matter remarked upon by Herodotus (II, 44), a contemporary of Thucydides, the Greek historian (471–401 B.C.) who was also very knowledgeable about the sea. Probably the close Egyptian association with sailors from the Eastern Mediterranean explains the motif of some of the many remains in what are considered to be old Levantine bases, recently found as far away as in various parts of Southern Africa. Using the radiocarbon dating technique it has been possible to date some of these bases from *c.* 4000 B.C., about the time the solar calendar was discovered by the Egyptians.[1]

Not content with what amounted to a trading monopoly in the western world, many Phoenicians were pirates and attacked the purely local ships trading between the various communities established around the Mediterranean littoral, and also vessels finally distributing treasures initially brought overland along caravan routes from the Far East. When they were finally driven out of Asia Minor by Darius the Persian, *c.* 550 B.C., they migrated to the Dodecanese Islands where they established the notorious Karian piracy, which was directed against the shipping of any nation attempting to break through their long-standing carrying monopoly.[2] Thereafter their distant overseas voyages must practically have ceased; anyway, there are no more references to such activities. Just how far these past voyages extended was never precisely known. Even the Greeks did not know until the fourth century B.C. about the existence of the British Isles so often visited by the Phoenicians.[3] Throughout the centuries they jealously guarded the secrets of their navigations and the ramifications of their trading activities, freely attacking any people whom they considered to be poaching on their preserves. Such a hostile attitude to others likely to encroach upon trade over which a monopoly was claimed was seen again during what might be imagined were more enlightened days in the 17th century. Then there were fights between traders in the Indian Ocean, even of the same nationality, when the various European Charter Companies, exercising monopolies granted by their home governments, strongly resisted anyone else being in those waters. Ordinary private traders resented this franchise, but were termed interlopers by the big concerns which employed every possible means to try to get rid of them.

Quite apart from that of the Levantines, later known as the Phoenicians, organised piracy was conducted on a large scale by the numerous island communities in the Aegean Sea and adjacent waters, which, obviously, must have greatly interfered with the local way of life. The pattern was very uniform: small boats pushed out to attack the becalmed or passing ship, the arrival of which was often signalled by look-outs. Ships which had anchored at sundown often moved after dark to a different place to lessen the risk of a night attack. Such a change of anchorage was quite easy, because ships then were propelled as much by sweeps (oars) as by sails. Some fifty years ago the late Professor Ormerod wrote a remarkably complete account of the life and nefarious activities of these ancient communities, including their migrations. Unfortunately, from much of this account it is difficult for the ordinary reader to benefit owing to numerous quotations in ancient Greek.[4] Although many of those distinct island peoples were but 50 miles apart, such a distance was quite something before the days of modern transport. In fact, even the large ships in later Roman times only moved about in the summer months because of the climatic and other navigational hazards. In one form or another piracy continued in this region until as late as the early 19th century, the final lairs being in the indented coast of Turkey in Asia, and in islands adjacent from which attacks could be made on the small merchantmen in the local Levant trade. The open boats traditionally used were difficult to catch, and the British frigate *Cambrian* was lost in 1829 on a reef near Crete trying to capture such a boat.

Around 1000 B.C. an important Phoenician settlement was made in Sardinia, where recent excavations by Professor Allbright strongly suggest that Tarshish, so famous for its shipping, and frequently mentioned in the Bible, was situated there. Hitherto the site of Tarshish has been a subject for much speculation.[5] That Sardinia could well be the place is confirmed by the reference in Isaiah (23, 6) to an island in connection with Tarshish; actually Herodotus (IV, 192) believed Tarshish to have been in Southern Spain, an opinion supported recently by Dr. Harden.[6]

Apart from their own special trading activities, it is evident that early Levantine mariners were, as it would be expressed nowadays, sea transport contractors to the Pharaohs, who were unable to build sea-going ships owing to the lack of suitable materials in Egypt. There was, however, Egyptian river-traffic in and around the Nile Delta, upon which there were frequent attacks in the region by Peoples of the Sea. Some of these came from various islands in the Eastern Mediterranean, and it is thought that many of them were in fact some of the people who in about

1400 B.C. had emigrated from the coast of Asia Minor to use Minos and adjacent islands as bases for their raids.[7]

Josephus refers to a special group of pirates who raided the Nile Delta about this time; but these were Etruscans, bold seamen from northern Italy called Tursha by the Egyptians. Apart from their dishonest maritime activities, they were dealers in tin, supplies of which they obtained in the southern parts of what is now France, after the metal had been brought overland from England, possibly to avoid clashes with the Phoenician merchants who transported their cargoes from the west of England to the Middle East by sea.[8] Somewhat later (c. 1200 B.C.), when the Libyans invaded Egypt, rovers from Libya and elsewhere took the opportunity for numerous raids on the shipping and shores of the Delta.

It is rather curious but the foregoing appear to be the few direct references to local piracy in Egyptian waters until comparatively recently. During the 17th and 18th centuries, Egypt, and Cairo in particular, became an important entrepôt in the Middle East trade with Europe. Vessels with valuable cargoes used to pass up and down the Nile, and were frequently attacked in the channels of the Delta by robbers who were expert swimmers. French travellers at the time remarked how these robbers approached victims by swimming underwater in the daytime, and how they used inflated goatskins by night to keep themselves afloat until they stormed a prize. The Arab sailors carried no firearms, and any Europeans who possessed them were welcome passengers because their ships were not attacked.

Round about 2000 B.C. there was a great increase in navigations by Mediterranean sailors both into the Indian Ocean and westwards into the Atlantic. These voyages may have been assisted by one of the regular upsurges in general world temperature (an event with a definite cycle, the last peak being about A.D. 500, permitting the great Norse voyages and migrations). The passage of ocean-going ships from the Mediterranean into the Red Sea and beyond was made possible at the time through the canal, cut by one of the Pharaohs named Sosostris, to connect a channel of the

Nile Delta with the Bitter lakes near Berket-el Hadj and so
to the Gulf of Suez. It is believed to have been 50 metres
wide and, apart from a few interruptions, was used until
the time of the Egyptian Ptolemies (300 B.C.). It was
repaired by Darius after the Persian occupation of Egypt,
c. 500 B.C., and a tablet erected by him reads, 'I commanded
to dig this canal from the stream flowing in Egypt, called
the Nile, to the sea which stretches from Persia. Then this
canal was dug as I commanded, and ships sailed from Egypt
through this canal to Persia according to my will'. Traces
of this canal are still visible.

Many Phoenician ships, engaged on what might be termed
the Indian Ocean run, used Ezion-Geber, situated at the
tip of the Gulf of Akaba, as their home port. Cargoes landed
there could be distributed conveniently overland to various
parts of Asia Minor. Another possible reason for the
importance of Ezion-Geber may have been that ships
using it did not have to run the gauntlet of the widespread
Mediterranean piracy. I have never seen more than passing
reference to piracy in the Red Sea in remote times; but
Roman ships in those waters were repeatedly attacked by
Arab pirates, so much so that police ships were commissioned
to provide some protection. This was necessary because the
Romans never controlled the coasts of the Red Sea, where
they developed a large trade into the Indian Ocean through
Myos Hormos, the port for Coptos which was then the
important commercial city of Upper Egypt. Pliny, who, as
well as being a famous scholar, was an officer in the Roman
navy, says how infested was the Red Sea, and that archers
were specially carried in merchantmen to beat off attacks.[9]
We learn from Tacitus, another Roman writer about this
time, how Arab pirates were dreaded because of the poisoned
arrows they used. Such fights between archers in merchantmen and pirate ships are interesting, because they provide
the first break in the 'immediately laying alongside and
boarding' method used in the past which, in fact, was
always employed to such effect until in the latter days of
piracy naval guns might sometimes be used to a limited
extent.

The celebrated Tarshish ships have been likened to East Indiamen, signifying a special kind of vessel, and it is quite obvious from the biblical and other references to them that they were outstanding. Of those based on Ezion-Geber, some were in the regional copper ore trade, but those of such great interest were the Tarshish ships, presumably based in Sardinia, which sailed freely in the Atlantic and returned with valuable cargoes of metals and other goods. Whether these ships fell victim to common piracy when actually in the Mediterranean is unknown; probably pirates dared not risk attacking them, just as they hesitated to attack East Indiamen in their prime. Still, their crews must have been pretty exhausted after long Atlantic voyages, a state to make the repelling of any attacks difficult.

As will be described in the next chapter, most of the treasures of all kinds being moved about the Mediterranean originated from remote places, and for centuries were brought home in Levantine bottoms. The voyages made by some of the early traders are quite astonishing. Herodotus (II, 2) records how ships chartered by Pharaoh Sosostris apparently started from Crete, sailed right round Africa in 2000 B.C., probably westabouts using the new 'Suez Canal', and taking advantage of the southerly currents down the East African coast. The currents in the Mozambique Channel are so strong that northward passages through this channel would have been extremely difficult for ships of the time; nevertheless, they managed to negotiate the contrary currents met off the Guinea Coast in the Atlantic and the north east trade winds of that region. The same historian (IV, 32) also refers to a similar voyage by Phoenician ships, much later, when on charter to Pharaoh Nacho, *c.* 600 B.C. This three-year voyage was definitely westabouts, and Herodotus remarks how 'the sun came to be seen on the right'. Such voyages were, however, only repeating distant navigations which the evidence indicates must have been regular practice a thousand years or more earlier.[10] The northerly position of the sun must, of course, have been noticed by the very early navigators, but, like so many other interesting things, went unrecorded.

Many years before this voyage it is clearly stated in 1 Kings, 10, 22 (1000 B.C.) that some treasure voyages by Tarshish ships took exactly three years. A ship propelled by oars and a square sail would have taken three years for a voyage round Africa collecting a cargo of gold, silver, ivory, apes and peacocks. In one year alone Solomon imported something like £10 million of gold. Think just of the amount of ivory needing to be shipped for building and all manner of purposes in what is now Palestine, during the reigns of David and Solomon. Of course, some of the ivory may have come from India, but it is doubtful whether India would have been able to supply the tonnage required. Furthermore, a round voyage to India took a year, whereas three years is the salient feature of the most important treasure voyages. Their true nature the reader must decide for himself. It is quite evident that the Levantine mariners were not the sort of people to sail round Africa, originally on behalf of any Pharaoh, and leave it at that if there was something to be gained; in fact, they established bases round the coast, where traces of Creto-Phoenician settlements still exist. Canon Haythornthwaite has often told me about his visits with the Abbe Bréuil to caves in the Brandburg and Obongo mountains in South West Africa, where numerous contemporary mural paintings and pottery remains can still be seen. These caves are now as much as fifty miles from the present coastline along which the sea is known to have been receding, due to well recognised causes, during the past three or four thousand years.[11] Though the earlier settlements show evidence of Egyptian influence it appears that later the Levantines and Phoenicians, working and trading very much for themselves, penetrated towards Central Africa, where what appear to be remains of this activity are to be found inland. So far these discoveries have been inadequately investigated because of the many practical difficulties involved. The sites are near some of the former great navigable rivers of Southern Central Africa, which drained into the Atlantic, but are now silted up. Further evidence of the extent of ancient European influence in Southern Africa is provided by certain Hottentot tribes, in whom features of their blood-groups suggest an admixture of European blood at some remote time.[12] Such settlements must have provided staging-points, during regular African trading voyages, for obtaining some of the commodities for which a big demand existed in Europe and Asia Minor: judging from the extent of piracy in the Mediterranean it is not difficult to imagine that some of the cargoes got into the wrong hands. Other European settlements, known to have existed both in the Azores and the Canary Islands, also provided useful ports of call on these long ocean voyages.

In the *Odyssey* there is direct reference to piracy in the story about the return of Odysseus to Ithaca after the Seige of Troy in 1100 B.C. Odysseus took so long on this journey—20 years—that his son, Telemachus, went to look for him. During this search he landed at Pylos, where he was hospitably welcomed. Nestor, King of Pylos, enquired if Telemachus 'were on some business or wandering at random over the sea as pirates who wander hazarding their lives and bringing evil to men of their lands'.[13]

Thucydides, writing about the Mediterranean pirate problem, describes how the Corinthians, who dominated the Peloponnesian peninsula from 700 B.C. onwards, used their navy (one of the first in history) to suppress the trouble in that region.[14]

During the Peloponnesian war in 424 B.C. the Spartans stationed a garrison on Kythera Island, near the channel of that name off the tip of Greece, to prevent its use by pirates wanting to interfere with their shipping. Because of its strategic importance, this same channel featured in naval operations in the two World Wars.

It is generally supposed that the Romans were able to achieve and maintain a satisfactory degree of law and order throughout their Empire. This was true on the whole in the vast land territories they occupied, but the situation was very different in the Mediterranean and adjacent waters. Plutarch, *c.* 50 B.C. (Caesar II, III), describes how no less a man than Julius Caesar, when a young man, was captured near Pharmacussa, where he was kept prisoner until ransomed for 50 shekels (about £50 in present-day values). After his release he collected some soldiers and traced his captors to their lair, where he overpowered and crucified them. Attacks on merchant shipping became so intense in the century immediately before A.D. 100 that the normal importation of wheat into Italy was reduced sufficiently to cause food shortages in Rome: pirates were to be found even around the mouth of the River Tiber. Shakespeare, in Anthony and Cleopatra (ii, 6), refers to the state of affairs then existing: '. . . and I must rid all the sea of pirates; then, to send measures of wheat to Rome; this greed upon, to part with unhackt edges, and bear back our targes undinted'. According to Plutarch there were then 1,000 pirate ships in commission at sea, making travelling in the Eastern Mediterranean particularly hazardous because of the bases both in Crete and on the Asiatic shores. We simply do not know how many trading vessels were attacked, but it is not difficult to imagine the effects of this widespread piracy on the general economy of the numerous seaboard communities dependent upon the sea for communications.

One of the more disgraceful events in Roman history concerns a successful pirate attack *c.* 70 B.C. on a Roman fleet off Sicily, resulting from the ineptitude of the Governor, an unpleasant man named Verres. Later he was due to be tried in Rome on a corruption charge when the great lawyer Cicero was the prosecutor. In the draft of his speech he referred to the disgraceful piracy in which Verres was involved.[15] In 67 B.C. a Bill was passed in the Roman Assembly conferring on Pompeius Magnus (Pompey) remarkable authority and the means to deal with the menace. The speech to the Assembly by Cicero advocating these measures still exists in his collected writings used by anyone learning Latin today. Pompey was the most distinguished general of his time, and as soon as he was provided with the necessary ships and men he conducted a ruthless and highly successful campaign. Not only did he free the seas, but raided the numerous pirate strongholds, many inhabitants of which were exiled from Asia Minor. What is so remarkable is that the whole complex operation was completed in a matter of months, providing an example of the wonderful

organisation of the Roman army. A few pirates must somehow have escaped Pompey, because in the *Monumentums
Aneyranium* the Emperor Augustus (44 B.C. - A.D. 14)
mentions, among other matters, how he finally cleared
the seas.

Many centuries later, Italians, or more correctly
Neapolitans, during the commercial expansion of that
kingdom, *c*. A.D. 1000, actually used pirates for their
personal advantage. At that time the Moors were starting
their Mediterranean piracy and required suitable ships and
sea stores, which they could obtain in Naples from greedy
traders in return for attacking ships belonging to other
merchants. More recently in the Middle Ages the Ottoman
Empire spread westwards and the rule of law was again
enforced, somewhat in Roman fashion, in occupied lands;
the bandits and other undesirables ashore would take to
piracy, thus adding to the number of maritime thieves
bedevilling the Mediterranean. They sought to capture
ships' crews and passengers, to be sold for slaves or to work
the Barbary galleys. So many Europeans met this fate that
when the Litany was compiled in the 16th century a prayer
was specially written: 'that it may please Thee to have mercy
on all prisoners, and captives. We beseech Thee to hear us,
good Lord'. In later days along the Turkish coast and
adjacent islands bordering the Aegean Sea, galleys were often
used in the manner of the Algerian corsairs. Though there
was an active trade between England and the Levant, English
ships seem to have escaped trouble, or at least there are no
detailed records available of any successful attacks on them.
Possibly these Aegean pirates had learnt by experience that
English ships were best left alone because of their armament.
For instance, one ship in that trade, *c*. 1600, *Hektor,* of
London, carried no less than 27 guns. On one voyage through
the islands she was menaced by four galleys which soon
sheered off when the fire power of their intended prize was
realised. One English ship, possibly from a Bristol Channel
port, was captured by the Turks early in the 17th century
and her crew made prisoners. There was a remarkable sequel.
A youth from Minehead in the crew was compelled to

become a Muslim, but eventually managed to escape and returned home clad in Turkish costume. This scandalised the local parishioners, who made him publicly renounce the apostasy which he had been obliged to accept. The lad, dressed as a Turk, was forced to stand in the parish church where a well-known West Country clergyman, Dr. Henry Byam, delivered what was nothing less than a long vitriolic sermon about his lapse from grace, including a remark about how he expected to attain Heaven in his unsanctified habit. The only redeeming feature of this deplorable public scene to readmit the youth to the Church was the final charge by Dr. Byam to the congregation, 'Let not what is said or done encourage you to rejoice in your neighbour's fall nor triumph in his misery'.

In restrospect all these ancient voyages are remarkable not only because of the simple type of vessel used but because of the many navigational problems involved. Most places around the Mediterranean could be reached by tedious voyages along the coastlines, but many others into the Atlantic and Indian Oceans were often out of sight of land. It is well known that the ancients had a profound knowledge of astronomy and the 'ordinances of the heavens'; also that they possessed instruments of considerable accuracy. Such knowledge could be applied to stellar navigation, and this may have been developed initially by learning to take short cuts at sea out of the sight of land. One can only speculate about the number of pirate ships attempting this kind of thing that were lost due to ignorance of navigation. Such was the fate in more recent times of many similar ships in other parts of the world, owing to proper navigators being rare and then often acting under duress.

Notes

1. *Science*, W. F. Libby, 116, 673. 1952.
2. Thucydides, I, 4, 5. (Jowett edn., 1881.)
3. *Aristotle*, De Mundo, 3.
4. *Piracy in the Ancient World, An Essay in Mediterranean History*, Ormerod, Henry A. Liverpool University Press, 1924.

5. *New Light on the Early History of Phoenician Colonisation.* Allbright, 1941.

6. *The Phoenicians.* Thomas and Hudson. London, 1962.

7. *Archaeological Classica,* IV. 72 ff. Stella, L. A.

8. *A Dictionary of the Bible.* 10th edn.

9. *Historia Naturalis,* VI. 101.

10. *South African Archaeology Bulletin, 8,* 91. Dart, Raymond A. December 1953.

11. *All the way to Abenab.* F. Haythornthwaite. Faber and Faber, 1953.

12. *Medical Bulletin,* Vol. III (1955), 144.

13. *Odyssey,* III, 51.

14. Thucydides. Jowett edn., 1881.

15. *Against Verres,* 11, V.

CHAPTER III

NORTHERN WATERS

THOUGH THE ORIGIN of the word 'viking' is unknown,
it came to be used to mean plundering, somewhat as a verb
'to go viking'. The Norsemen were plunderers, with cruelties
hardly equalled by any other people. They were said to go
berserk, an expression implying an extreme degree of violence
still used in this sense. In the days of their greatest activity
about the ninth century, not only in Northern Europe, but
further afield, the Norse waregars (lit. seafaring people),
were known as Russes or Russians, according to Müller
writing in the early 18th century.[1] After they had crossed
the Baltic and conquered the surrounding countries they
spread through what is now Russia, which derived its name
from these Norse invaders. Territories as far off as Ireland
were used as bases for piracy in Western Europe; old bases
recently discovered in County Mayo and elsewhere are being
examined at the time of writing. In the Mediterranean,
settlements were established for about 100 years in North
Africa from which to attack the local shipping, but they
were finally expelled in A.D. 534 by Belisarius, one of the
last great Romans.

Well after the days of the original Norsemen, two Norse
pirates of Germanic origin, named Godekins and Stertebekers,
were renowned in the 14th century for their depredations
in and around the North Sea. There they not only attacked
merchantmen, but made forays ashore, the most notable
being an attack on the Swedish town of Norbern, which they
plundered and held the leading citizens to ransom. On one
occasion they sailed down the English Channel as far west as
Plymouth, from where they took a prize.

Norse influence provided the original stimulus for most of the piracy around the British Isles, which by the Middle Ages had become serious, just at a period when English sea trade with Europe was thriving. There is an amusing story about a party of Flemish merchants crossing the Channel in the 12th century to buy English wool, and with whom were a number of monks. The ship was menaced by pirates, much to the dismay of the merchants, who assured the monks that if they were saved all of their wealth would go to Our Lady of Laon. Actually nothing untoward happened and everybody arrived safely in England, when the vows were conveniently forgotten.

The Hebrides or Orkneys might, at first sight, be regarded as places remote from European trade routes. But it was common practice for a very long time for European ships leaving ports around the North Sea to make passage into the Atlantic by the northern route, where there was more sea room than in the English Channel. The Channel was often difficult to clear because of the prevailing westerly winds. While it was known that important bases existed in the Hebrides, and the Orkneys, who could do anything about them? There was then no regular navy from which ships could be detached to police the coasts, and no action from the shore side was possible owing to lack of road access. We know from the story in Southey's *Inchcape Rock* that retribution caught up with at least one of the rovers operating off the Scottish coast. Judging from the context, Arbroath (Aberbrothok) was Sir Ralph's home port which, considering the importance of that place at the time, indicates the open way in which piracy was conducted. The Abbey of Arbroath was closed in 1547 after the assassination of the last abbot, the notorious Cardinal Beaton, so the events described in the poem must have occurred before then. For the benefit of many who since schooldays may only recall a somewhat earthy version of this poem, it is reproduced in Appendix I as originally written.

The most notorious of the Hebridean pirates was Rory MacNeil, from the island of Barra, whose ramifications extended as far as Ireland. One of the first uses of the now common expression 'by hook or by crook', but less forceful in meaning, concerned this man. James VI (later James I of England) wished to interview MacNeil after formal protests from London about his attacks on English shipping. The courier with the royal summons was instructed to use any method (by hook or by crook) to bring the miscreant to Edinburgh.

The Orkneys were in the news as late as 1724 in connection with the activities of Captain John Gow, who provided the basis for Captain Cleveland, a character in Sir Walter Scott's novel *The Pirate*. Gow was second mate in a merchantman, *George,* when he and others on board mutinied while in European waters, an unusual event so near home, ostensibly owing to the bad conditions on board and a miserly captain. Gow turned pirate, and after capturing various ships, went to the Orkneys to sell his stolen cargoes. Many of his men deserted and Gow himself had to run for it, and, after various vicissitudes on the Scottish mainland, he was finally captured. He stood his trial at Newgate in London, where he refused to say anything. To make him plead he was ordered to be pressed, the only judicial torture then permitted. It consisted of stretching out the prisoner on the floor and adding increasing weights to a board laid over his body. Gow responded to this persuasion as desired, but was hanged nevertheless.

The geographical features of the Irish coastline, particularly in the south, provided admirable lairs. They were used to some extent by locals, but much more by men from other countries waiting to attack the increasingly busy shipping in the Western Approaches. These troublesome visitors were much in evidence in late Tudor and early Stuart times, when trade was very brisk between places like Cork (Carcaigh) and the Biscayan ports and the Iberian peninsula. Because of its situation Broadhaven was for a long time the most popular pirate base. It was there that a local woman named Grace O'Malley achieved notoriety as a chief; and, late in life, when widowed, she was received by Queen Elizabeth I in London. Another place called Beerhaven was popular owing to the readiness of a local Irish peer, O'Sullivan, Prince of Beer and Bantry, to buy stolen cargoes.

Attacks on merchantmen became sufficiently intense to restrict the Irish export trade, when much was being done in the time of James I (1603-1625) to promote this trade in order to help restore the debased currency of that country. Things got so bad that on instructions from London, a special search was made from sea by Sir William Monson, and Broadhaven, still frequently used, was cleared up. By that time affairs were directed by a local man named Cormac who obviously had made a good thing out of piracy. It is evident that for many years local inhabitants in the south of Ireland derived much benefit from pirated goods, much as people round the coasts of England benefited from smuggling a century or two later.

But the bad old ways returned, and, by 1611, Dutch shipping was suffering so severely that the Dutch government had to send men-of-war of its own to deal with a menace nobody else would do anything about. Even after this effort the foreign pirates returned, including a contingent of Algerian corsairs, some of whom even raided Baltimore and carried off many of the inhabitants as prisoners into slavery. In Northern Ireland small-scale piracy had been going on for years, but nothing was done to stop it until Thomas Wentworth, later Earl of Strafford, that celebrated Governor of Ireland, took it upon himself in 1636 to have pirates of any description driven away from the Irish coasts. After this there was little further trouble.[2, 3]

On the south coast of England, ships from the Cinque Ports were not above sallying forth to plunder passing vessels. So did groups from Poole and, further west, from the Scillies, which provided favourite bases because of their strategic position at the mouth of the Channel. The French, too, were to be found in the Channel for what could be picked up, and as early as the beginning of the 12th century they even landed on the Roseland peninsula in Cornwall, a place now well known to tourists. St. Anthony's church and monastery there were originally the Church of the Priory and Convent of St. Mary de Valle, which were raided and destroyed very much in the way the Norsemen used to treat priories 500 years earlier. St. Mary's was later rebuilt and restored by the Bishop of Exeter in 1124. Conditions in the English Channel were at their worst later on in the 14th century at about the time of the French wars which culminated in the battle of Crécy. The military activities ashore gave the numerous pirates on both sides of the Channel free range on all shipping—indeed, historians have designated this period as the 'pirate war'. In 1340 French pirates even raided and burnt Teignmouth, and afterwards made an unsuccessful attack on Plymouth.

Today it is difficult to think of Poole Harbour, with its crowded anchorages and built-up foreshore, as a lair. But it is necessary to appreciate what the neighbourhood of Poole was like in Tudor times. Study of a contemporary map (Plate 2) reveals that apart from the small town of Poole, the whole region was desolate and ideally suited to the requirements of men like Harry Paye, who made the Harbour his headquarters in the 1500s.[4] Later, when Poole harbour became untenable, its physical features made it a popular centre for smugglers.

Lundy Island, that rocky island in the Bristol Channel, would not at first sight appear to be a very propitious place for gangs, but it is well known locally how freely it was used because of its situation, although, except in fine weather, it is a grim place with strong tides sweeping past. There is no proper harbour, only a roadstead and a landing beach, so exactly how operations were conducted must remain speculative. The first seamen to visit Lundy regularly were the Vikings, whose craft could readily be beached. Later, as the use of ordinary sailing ships developed, those trading mainly in and around the Bristol Channel were designed to enable them to be beached because of the extreme rise and fall of the tides, as much as 12 metres in some places.

Reliable information about early happenings on Lundy dates from when it was already owned by the de Marisco family, and Sir Jordan de Marisco quarrelled with Henry II (1154–1189). Later his son William, who succeeded to the title, took to piracy, possibly to show his contempt for authority, preying on ships in the Western Approaches; he and other inhabitants of the island subsisted mainly on the spoils. Sir William was arrested in 1242 and after being dragged from Westminster to the Tower of London, was hanged, drawn and quartered. According to Laurence (*A History of Capital Punishment*) this was the first application of the horrible punishment used so often in later years for prisoners deemed necessary to be specially humiliated in death. A direct descendant of the de Mariscos still lives on Lundy.

After this the island had various ups and downs, but was in the news again in the time of Henry VIII (1509-1547) when a French gang established itself; the gang, somewhat surprisingly, was driven out by fishermen from Clovelly. Because of Lundy's merits as a base, pirates of various nationalities, including Algerian corsairs, were soon back again in operation. In the early 1600s an Englishman named Salkeld was even due to be crowned the Pirate King of Lundy; however, this coronation did not take place due to prompt action by the mayor of Barnstaple. In those days Barnstaple was an important English port whose shipping was constantly being attacked. As late as 1663, Frenchmen under a Captain Pressoville were in occupation, but Charles II got rid of them soon after the Restoration.

Two other islands in the Bristol Channel, Sully and Barry islands, near Cardiff, were also used for attacks on Bristol shipping, and these later attained notoriety as smugglers' haunts. Such past events are hard to believe when you think of Barry Island today with its fun fair and suchlike. As far as I know the other two islands in the Bristol Channel, Flat Holm and Steep Holm, only feature once in pirate history, probably because landing on these is so difficult. Some Danish pirates driven from Watchet and Porlock took refuge on Steep Holms [*sic*] which, being steep, could be defended better than Flat Holm. But worse than any assault they might have had to repulse was the fact that they starved to death.[5]

Having to run the gauntlet of the Bristol Channel and the Western Approaches, Bristol ships from earliest times always suffered badly, and even after pirates around the British Isles were cleared up they were still at risk on the Guinea coast and in the New World. Bristol ships, and, somewhat later, Liverpool ships specialised in a triangular run from England: to West Africa to load slaves, from thence to the West Indies, and finally back home with a cargo of sugar and rum. Like other merchantmen on deep sea voyages they were armed, though details of this are lacking. However, some indication of their special armament is the old powder jetty at the side of the Avon Gorge leading to Bristol. Because of the quantity of gunpowder carried it was considered unsafe for these ships to enter the port of Bristol before their powder had been discharged. Special provision for doing so was available at the jetty, the remains of which still exist, with the derrick used to hoist the powder barrels; ships usually had about 10 to 15 tons on board. Outward-bound the vessels simply re-loaded. A Bristol pilot, whose ancestors for several centuries had been pilots, once told me that there was no other port where such precautions against explosion risk were deemed necessary.

Apparently the east coast of England does not feature much in the pirate story because of its configuration and because it was not a very convenient place from which to attack regular shipping lanes. Still, there must have been other incidents of the kind in which Woodbridge featured, as described on page 101. A further reason for freedom from much bother may spring from the fact that for a very long time most of the King's ships, or men-of-war, were stationed in and around the Thames Estuary, and so could act as police in the North Sea. Perhaps the most remarkable story of eastern England concerns the River Yare, of all places, in the late 18th and early 19th centuries. Along this river was conveyed the extensive two-way commercial traffic between Norwich and Great Yarmouth. The craft mainly used, and often in charge of only one man, were the Norfolk wherries of some forty tons burthen, propelled by a large single fore-and-aft sail and by the appropriate use of the tide. In those days the river ran through a sparsely populated and desolate region, and cargo robberies were frequent, despite the handsome rewards offered for information by the merchants who suffered so badly—some as much as by nearly £1,000 annually. Even some of the wherrymen themselves were not averse to a bit of peculation by short-weight deliveries, usually detected. Occasionally the regular thieves were caught and sentenced to transportation, but many were not caught, and their depredations continued until the railway came.

Ordinary history books describe the political or official relations between England and Spain in Tudor times, but fail to say much about the resentment by English folk of the way Spain was attempting to dominate and exploit so much of the world to the exclusion of other Europeans. This resentment was aggravated by the fact that Spanish activities received papal support and the horrors of the Inquisition. Feeling that riches available overseas were being monopolised by Spain was particularly increased among west of England fishermen whose European trade had declined as one result of the Reformation. They were ready to attack Spanish ships on the high seas carrying what were regarded as ill-gotten gains. Apart from the likely material gains from attacking them, the Spaniards' inhuman behaviour to ordinary seamen, particularly Englishmen whom they regarded as heretics, caused men in high places in the time of Edward VI (1547–1553) who were unable to persuade the government to move, to take it upon themselves to obtain the redress by private enterprise. Thus it came about that even Sir Thomas Seymour, who was Lord High Admiral (a chief executive appointment not finally abolished until the present century) gave up the unequal struggle with the government and bought the Scilly Isles, where he set up as a pirate chief with Spanish ships as the objective. And he was not alone in adopting this new life. Men from the west of England in particular joined in, the Strangeways, the Tremaynes, the Carews, and others with family names still known today. But where could they get their ships and stores? These were obtained in France of all places, simply because Henry II of France hated Spain so bitterly; he hated heresy, but he hated Spain more. One extraordinary character must have been Thomas Stukeley, who became associated with Sir Thomas Seymour after he opened up in the Scilly Isles. In due course Stukeley bought a largish ship, ostensibly to go to Florida to start a colony. No sooner had he sailed from Plymouth than he announced to his crew that the trans-Atlantic voyage was off and that he was going to take to piracy. This he did, operating from a northern Irish creek, where an Ulsterman called Shan O'Neill acted as his agent ashore. Stukeley came to a miserable end, more or less as a refugee on Lundy Island with the pirates usually found there. Seymour himself fared worse; he was finally caught and executed.

With men from good families as leaders coastal seamen of all types, sanctified by religious fervour, flocked to the new life. In so doing a race of magnificent seamen with fast ships developed, who were later already trained to save this country from invasion in 1588. To put the matter simply: pirates in peace-time became the armed forces of the Crown in war. The ferocity of these Tudor privateers, pirates, call them what you will, was exacerbated by the continuous Spanish brutality to English prisoners. One basically respectable Englishman, one of the Cobhams, attacked a Spanish ship in the Channel with 40 prisoners on board on their way to Spain to be tormented by the Inquisition. After capturing the Spanish ship and rescuing the prisoners, Cobham had the Spanish crew sewn up in their own main-sail and heaved overboard. This strange parcel was finally washed ashore and there was a frightful row, but nothing came of it. French rovers would go so far as to chase Spanish ships into English waters, and one even right into Falmouth harbour, but because of the English feeling toward Spain no one bothered about international legal niceties involved by such an event.

While it is difficult to reconcile sea robbery with anything to do with Christianity we must remember that piracy against Spain was for a long time regarded as a religious crusade, to the extent that later on it was common practice for pirates in the New World to hold Divine Service before starting a raid. Be this as it may, Professor Ormerod (*loc. cit.*) has drawn attention to the strange rites and sacrifices made by Mediterranean pirates several thousand years ago; also observances, Moslem in character, before raids in the Aegean in the 12th century.

The strangest pirate fleet of all was one based at Dover, during the Spanish domination of the Netherlands in the 16th century. This fleet was predominantly Flemish, together with a number of Englishmen, under the command of a Fleming, Count de la Marc. These ships played havoc with Spaniards passing anywhere near, and the stolen cargoes were regularly sold in Dover market. The prizes were ships trading with the Spanish Netherlands and also supply ships for the Spanish army stationed there. Even the Spanish prisoners were publicly auctioned in Dover for prices related to the ransom money particular individuals would probably fetch. When a change of scene was thought desirable, some of these Dover-based ships would sail off to the Spanish coast and raid towns at will, after which chalices from pillaged churches were used as goblets at feasts on board ship when toasts were drunk to the raiders' success. Although the matter is outside the subject of this book, it is of interest to think that this queer fleet at Dover helped to protect England from a possible Spanish invasion before the Armada.

European public opinion finally compelled Elizabeth I, in 1572, to order the Flemish fleet out of Dover, being declared *gueux de mer* (rascals of the sea); so Count de la Marc urgently needed a new Channel base. He decided to make a surprise attack on the Dutch coast, where he occupied Brill after capturing this port from the Spaniards. This success resulted in widespread revolt against the Spaniards in the Netherlands and their ultimate expulsion from the region.[6] Thus the Holland we know today became re-established and, in retrospect, it is extraordinary that the prime movers in the relieving fleet were nothing more than pirates. The zeal behind these Dutchmen was Calvinistic Protestantism, a zeal as great, if not greater, than that of English seamen in those days, who however much they suffered at sea, were not persecuted in a homeland occupied by a foreign power. Such a background must leave its mark on any nation. So, in the next century when the Dutch settled in South Africa, the early colonists were imbued with a religious fervour which has influenced South African politics up to the present day, something indeed from which the apartheid doctrine has sprung.

Although the Dutch have always been a maritime nation, Dutchmen, with certain notable exceptions, did not readily take to piracy. One reason perhaps was because few Dutch seamen ever lacked a berth; both in war and peace their fishing industry was continuously prosperous as well as ordinary trade. The Dutch West Indies Company founded in 1621 must have possessed ideas of its own because one of its captains, Piet Hein, in 1628 successfully attacked the Spanish treasure fleet and seized plunder worth about seven million pounds. The next year the company paid a dividend of 50 per cent.!

Over the years one thing with far-reaching consequences on the whole of British maritime life and practice, whether lawful or unlawful, was the emphasis on the speed and handiness of English ships. This prevented their capture even when out-numbered. Ocean-going ships, particularly in Tudor times, were built, too, with a loving care which has hardly been known since; the shipwrights and riggers ashore realised after the Reformation, that the only men who could keep the Papists away from England were the seamen who ran all the risks, so that it was up to those in safe jobs ashore to ensure that nothing was ever scamped or neglected. Something else was the early emphasis on good gunnery; thus it came about that English ships came to be fought with guns rather than with the hoards of soldiers customary on board continental ships, when the one idea was to lay along-side and board an enemy from 'castles'. Pirate crews often boarded their opponents, but not in this way—they used a special method to be described later, a method also used sometimes by successful French privateers.

An important way of increasing the speed and handiness of English ships was first made possible in the time of Henry VIII, probably by John Fletcher of Rye, who was mayor in 1545.[7] This was the fore-and-aft rig as known today, though initially it was only used in small vessels.

While it is true that the Arabs first discovered it was possible to beat to windward, this was achieved by the lateen sail characteristic of dhows. Fletcher's discovery was a revolution in European ship design because it became easy to beat to windward, something of which the Channel pirates were not slow to take advantage, since they could literally make circles round the conventional clumsy merchantmen.

The final vindication of the new maritime practices developed by Englishmen was demonstrated when the Armada arrived; the Spanish ships were out-manoeuvred and out-ranged, so much so that the Spaniards thought it unfair and even cowardly for our ships not to allow themselves to be boarded. While English seamen accepted their responsibility for the nation, they always had the fear of being taken prisoner. The most important effect of all they did was the clear demonstration to the world that Spanish seapower was not invincible and that their ships could be attacked without hesitation. After the defeat of the Armada most European nations joined in the quest for loot from the Spaniards who were thought, not unreasonably, to have obtained much of their treasures by stealing from the original inhabitants of the countries Spain was colonising. But gradually the new and growing race of European pirates in home waters did not confine their attentions only to Spanish vessels, and a less tolerant public attitude developed to the whole business. Probably because of this attitude the chief centre shifted to the New World, where it flourished until the end of the 17th century. The constant European wars involving France and Spain were purely military affairs ashore; neither government bothered very much about what was going on at sea.

The Spanish complaint that their not being allowed to board in a fight with the English was unfair must have been regretted when the pirates in the New World, of most European nationalities and of whom many were English, boarded Spanish ships almost at will. Due to a feature in their design, certain Spanish ships were easy prey for a determined boarding party. This was most noticeable in ships built overseas, primarily for local voyages between the new towns and cities springing up; further, not all were fitted with the guns with which the merchantmen of any nationality were usually armed. In locally-built ships that did carry guns, these were not arranged to fire through gun-ports from which they could be withdrawn inboard for loading. Instead, they were mounted on platforms outside the gun-ports where they had to be re-loaded. This meant that the exposed gunners could easily be killed by well directed small-arms fire during the first stage of any attack on the ship. Even gunners in ships with ordinary gun-ports could be at risk from determined small-arms fire. Since in sea battles the men matter just as much as the ship, it is worth mentioning that in the Spanish ships trading locally, both in the New World and in other overseas territories, there were few pure-bred Spaniards apart from the officers; crews usually consisted of half-castes and 'Indians'. The reason was that as a nation the thought of being seamen was beneath their dignity. The exceptions from this attitude were the men hailing from the Biscayan ports, who were magnificent seamen, and the men instrumental in maintaining Spanish sea power while it lasted.

Notes

1. *De originibus Gentis et Nominis Russorum.*
2. From the private history of a local family.
3. Irish Archaeological Society 29, 1841.
4. *Harry Paye.* Herbert S. Carter, J. Looker Ltd. 1934.
5. A. S. Chronicles MSS. B.C.D.
6. *English History Review.* J. B. Black. 1932.
7. *History of Rye.* Chapter 3.

CHAPTER IV

THE NEW WORLD

PIRACY IN SEAS DISTANT from Europe really started when the Elizabethans demonstrated how Spanish treasure ships and strongholds in the New World could be attacked successfully. The exploits of Drake, Hawkins and other distinguished men are common knowledge. Once such a pattern was set it was only a matter of time before the main emphasis on piracy was to be found in the New World, a situation lasting for about one hundred and fifty years. As European waters were policed better, it became wiser to seek adventures in less hazardous places and where the best prizes existed which, in due course, were sought by men from all European countries.

No other region of the world has provided a greater wealth of pirate stories than the Caribbean and its adjacent waters. Many of them have been written up and are so familiar that there is no need to repeat them. But the origin and the way of life of the men involved provide a fascinating study, and, later, an attempt has been made to portray these human factors. The real story of the buccaneers is somewhat at variance with that commonly accepted; by no means all those active in the Caribbean were really buccaneers. As mentioned previously these were a race of men apart, mostly of French extraction. Their full story is told in Chapter XII.

Throughout the 17th century maritime conditions in the Caribbean and along the Pacific Coast of Central and South America must have resembled those in the Mediterranean, when Pompey the Roman was ordered to clear things up. There were periods during which pirates held command of the sea locally, but at least they did not precipitate a food shortage ashore as happened in Italy in Roman times. The people living in coastal settlements, however, did sometimes become very short of ordinary domestic supplies owing to the trade ships being captured or frightened away. Because pirates laid considerable stress on reasonably good relations with colonists and other local inhabitants they would provide them, when possible, with domestic commodities they might otherwise be unable to obtain.

It is surprising that for so long European governments, despite their frequent preoccupation with continental wars, bothered so little about the general state of lawlessness overseas; but pirate ships owed little or no allegiance to any government, irrespective of the nationality of the captains. As for the crews, men came from anywhere. Even the various Charter Companies holding franchises in the New World appear to have turned a blind eye to local events and, on occasions, were not too scrupulous to benefit from spoils (mostly of Spanish origin) obtained by very questionable means.

In the days of overseas expansion by European Powers, there were times when things must have been very topsy-turvy. Take the case of Henry Morgan, about whom so much is known. Here was a man originally nothing better than a thief. In 1671, by which time Jamaica was a thriving English colony, Morgan heard of a pending Spanish attack and informed the Governor. As a result the Council of Jamaica authorised him to harry the Spaniards as he liked, so he mounted his successful and lucrative attack on Panama which put a stop to any Spanish aggression for the time being. Thereafter Morgan became respectable. It was an extraordinary situation how this man, untrustworthy even to his own shipmates, could ultimately become Governor of Jamaica and win a knighthood.

Sir Hans Sloane, the distinguished doctor and naturalist, whose name is perpetuated by a street and a square in London, visited Jamaica when Morgan was there. He had various conversations with him, mentioned in a book he wrote about his visit to the West Indies.[1] It is fascinating to read his remark 'as Sir Henry Morgan often said' how

Borequen or Crab Island (now called Vicques), lying between Puerto Rico and Santa Cruz (St. Croix), came to be used as a pirate base. This particular story illustrates what could go on overseas when the nations involved were not even at war with each other.

What happened was that two English (pirate) ships went one day to Crab Island and simply carried off all the 150 Spanish inhabitants, men, women, and negroes, and replaced them with English settlers. History does not relate the fate of the prisoners, but by current practice the negroes would have been put to work in the raiding ship as personal servants of the crews, or made into ordinary seamen, a calling in which many negroes could become very proficient. Some time later an unpleasant Englishman, whose name is uncertain, barbarously attacked the new settlers, having masqueraded as a Spaniard to avoid undue alarm to his intended victims. Local peace was finally restored when Captain Sharp, famous for his Pacific privateering exploits partly in association with William Dampier, became commander of the island and adapted the place for his own purposes. One wonders what else Morgan told the doctor, because he was one of the few outstanding captains who survived to tell the tale of what rovers did; what a tale it must have been.

Eventually in 1689 there was a local edict in the Caribbean outlawing piracy. The past deeds of men willing to turn over a new leaf would be forgotten, and as for the others . . . well! Many who did not want to change their occupation transferred their activities to the Indian Ocean, making their headquarters in Madagascar, increasingly being used as a base for attacks on ships in the Far East trade. The situation remained thus well into the 18th century, and for the best part of a century little could be done to stop it, because all European navies were either busy fighting each other, or were otherwise occupied. On the way to Madagascar some migrants operated for a while along the Guinea Coast of West Africa, causing a lot of trouble among ships on the first leg of the regular triangular run between Europe, the West Indies and back to Europe. Chapter XI describes the sort of things that happened on the Guinea Coast. With the arrival of the displaced persons from the New World in Madagascar these skilled reinforcements led to a serious state of affairs developing in the Indian Ocean.

Some of those affected by the Caribbean edict of 1689 moved northwards and plagued shipping in the waters along the New England coast. New operational bases to do this were set up either in the Bahamas, or in Newfoundland, where the numerous sea inlets provided sheltered anchorages, and the notorious fogs provided extra screening from the curious. According to Captain Charles Johnson, writing at the time, there were as many as 2,000 men engaged in piracy along the American seaboard, and the coast was not finally made safe until well into the 1700s.[2] Shortly before the final clearance there was an unexpected upsurge in lawlessness. This was mainly due to the increased restrictions imposed by their home governments on trading by European colonists in the New World; since Spain had the largest colonial territories people in these were most affected. The result of the various restrictions was that large-scale smuggling started, and in an attempt to stop it the Spanish government commissioned a number of privateers, but they seem to have been used only for a short time. The European merchants engaged in smuggling suffered badly at first from the Spanish privateers, and they organised reprisals, using privately commissioned ships for this purpose. These ships were not proper privateers, under Letters of Marque from any government, and soon they started to attack not merely the Spanish ships, as intended, but ships of any nationality. Things got so bad that the English government on its part issued a proclamation about the illegality of what was going on.[3]

Another reason for this final upsurge was the fact that the Bahamas provided such a good base for operations. Many years earlier the island had been used by pirates, but their popularity had declined. Always the Bahamas had been regarded as English territory; however, compared with other islands they were poor. Still, Charlestown (later named Nassau in honour of Dutch William, King William III) in New Providence was anchorage for shipping of all nationalities, and no one put awkward questions to pirates and others of that ilk. On two occasions the Spaniards destroyed the settlement, and when, in 1704, a new governor arrived from England to take office he found the place depopulated and desolate. So all he could do was to return to England. Pirates then moved in wholesale and became such a serious menace to shipping that Bristol merchants in particular, trading with the West Indies, persuaded the British government to resume proper control of New Providence, and Captain Woods Rogers was appointed governor.

Woods Rogers had distinguished himself as a privateer captain in the Pacific where, among other exploits, he had rescued Alexander Selkirk from Juan Fernandez, so providing Daniel Defoe with the basis for the Robinson Crusoe story. Woods Rogers had only 100 men with him to re-establish law and order when he arrived in 1718; nevertheless, he had the whole place under control within a month. As a temporary measure Royal Pardon was extended to some 2,000 pirates who surrendered, but some of those who did not were captured, and 10 were executed after trial in New Providence. These convictions were possible because former associates turned King's Evidence. The executions were watched by a large crowd in which there were many one-time pirates, but, as someone remarked, 'They never thought to have seen the time when ten such men as they should be tied up and hanged like dogs and four hundred of their sworn friends and companions quietly standing by to behold the spectacle'. A voice from the crowd called upon them to repent of their misdeeds. 'Yes', answered one, 'I do heartily repent, I repent I had not done more mischief and that we did not cut the throats of them that took us; and I am extremely sorry that you arn't hanged as well as we are' (quoted by Johnson). As a matter of interest, it was Woods Rogers who organised the Representative Assembly for the Bahamas in 1729, one of the first British territories overseas to enjoy what was basically parliamentary government.

Piracy in the New World during the 17th century might be regarded at first sight as an event only important at the time, but it so interrupted central Spanish government control of overseas possessions that it provided one pre-disposing cause of the break-up of the Spanish Empire.

Notes

1. *Voyage to the Islands of Madeira, Barbados, Nevis, St. Christopher and Jamaica.* 1707.
2. *General History of the Pyrates.* Charles Johnson, 1724.
3. Given by George I at Hampton Court, 5 September 1717.

CHAPTER V

THE   ORIENT

CONSIDERING the extensive trading up and down the Red Sea and along its coasts in ancient times, it is difficult to imagine that this went on without attracting pirates. Certainly we know definitely that, by Roman times, this had become such a menace that special ships were provided to police the area, though the Romans never occupied the Red Sea coasts. It is believed that many of the deep water inlets along the Arabian coast provided, for a very long time, the bases for raiders backed by the towns and settlements situated on these inlets. Due to climatic changes which, over the centuries, have entirely altered the character of the western Arabian seaboard, traces of those settlements have mostly disappeared. Along the southern coast of Arabia, facing the Gulf of Aden and the Arabian Sea, which were well provided with suitable harbours, conditions remained favourable for pirates who attacked the increasing sea-borne trade to India and the Far East. By the time the Portuguese came on the scene in the 15th century, Southern Arabia was known as The Pirate Coast. In attempts to combat the menace the Portuguese and, later, the English, established bases in Muscat, but any control that could be exerted was limited and local pirates came and went more or less as they pleased. When not pirating, the same men engaged in the local slave trade from Africa to Arabia, a trade only finally suppressed by the British Navy. In 1695 a one-time privateer captain named Kidd was specially retained to try and curtail piracy in the Gulf of Aden and the Arabian Sea. He was provided with a galley, *Adventure,* a ship highly suitable for a mission of this nature since she was propelled largely by sweeps which made her very independent of wind when following quarries in awkward places. Kidd was not very successful and finally betook himself to the New World, where he became a free-lance adventurer with unscrupulous habits.

Soon after its incorporation (in 1600) the English East India Company attempted to open up trade by sea with Persia (Iran) and started trade posts at Basra and Bushire. It was an unrewarding exercise owing to the frequent attacks on ships in the Persian Gulf and off the Oman coast, so the venture was practically abandoned. However, towards the end of the 18th century renewed efforts were made to promote the trade, but again it was harassed by piracy more rampant than ever, and mostly organised by Europeans operating from Madagascar which had been transformed into a pirate island.

Madagascar might be a British possession today inasmuch that as early as 1640 English traders there drew attention to its strategic value; nothing was done about it. Then two years later Cardinal Richelieu, on behalf of Louis XIV, granted a French 'Captain de la Marine' the sole concesssion to colonise and trade: French settlers arrived in 1643, founding Fort Dauphin as a supply base for French East Indiamen. Later, due to the ineptitude of the French governor, the Malagasy revolted; thereafter pirates came and went unhindered and were able to dispose of cargoes of general merchandise at leisure. Happenings in Madagascar have been well described by both French and English historians.[1, 2]

As men of many nationalities increasingly made their headquarters in the island they established good relations with the native inhabitants, an association that was fostered by the ease with which the coastal population could obtain clothing and firearms from them. In the course of time some Madagascan pirates were not content to confine their activities to attacking ships, but engaged in the profitable African negro slave trade to the Near East. Cargoes of slaves were obtained from Mozambique, many of whom were taken to Madagascar for onward routing. This particular activity enraged the Malagasy who turned the skills learnt from pirates against their teachers and, as a result, some bases around the coast became isolated communities only approachable by sea. Since the coastline is 2,000 miles long there was plenty of room for these settlements. Time healed the breach with the local people, and, with help from the Europeans, what could be called the Malagasy Kingdoms became established. The most important of them were on the east coast. From one of these a man named Ratsinilaha, son of an English pirate, actually went to England to be educated. On his return he married a princess of the Zafinelramissa tribe, and ultimately became head of one of what later came to be known as the pirate republics. He died in 1750.

Pirates from Madagascar ranged all over the Indian Ocean and even into the Pacific. In the book about his explorations on behalf of the East India Company, Captain Forrest refers to English pirates operating around New Guinea and the Moluccas in the sense that they formed part of the accepted local order of things. This same writer particularly emphasises the risks to single ships from attacks by Papuans.[3]

Nearly two hundred years ago, Voltaire, the Frenchman, summarised the final position in these words: 'The pirates of the European and American seas were organised and were in Madagascar and its waters making the last stand against the lawful government of the world'.[4]

In and around the China Sea what might be called deep sea piracy was a fairly late development, mainly because of the degree of law and order maintained by the Chinese government ashore and over the waters where it exercised jurisdiction. Generally speaking the Chinese never wanted foreign commodities they could not produce from their own vast natural resources, and being inherently honest as a nation were not interested in stolen goods. This was a situation quite unlike that in Western Europe where the inhabitants had necessarily to import much of their requirements, particularly luxury goods, and if at times these happened to have been smuggled or came from other questionable sources no questions were asked.

Despite the vast land mass of China few countries have a longer coastline, and the Chinese have always been fine seamen; indeed, they were using compasses long before they were known in Europe. These men must have been skilled to navigate as far as they did in junks rigged only with plain pole masts and matting sails. In the 14th, 15th and 16th centuries such vessels regularly reached the Persian Gulf, the east coast of Africa, and even Madagascar, with cargoes of silk and ceramics for final distribution in Arab dhows. Apart from risks incurred in the Arabian Sea it is apparent that these Chinese ships were at risk nearer home from the Cantonese, because in 1557 the Chinese government leased Macao to the Portuguese in return for their help in suppressing piracy. Even the Portuguese had their troubles, because after converting the nearby island of Lappa into a well-laid-out residential place, they had to abandon it because of raids by pirates. In the south around the Pearl River the Cantonese formed a community of their own, and were never regarded by the central government in Peking as very law-abiding. It was from this region that most, if not all, Chinese pirates originated, a situation lasting well into the present century.

Once European East Indiamen regularly sailed into the Indian Ocean, Chinese ships usually terminated their voyages in Malaya, where transhipments took place. Those junks that went to Malaya did not always return to China, but often sailed on afterwards between the Celebes and Indo-China, somewhat as local traders, due to the limited market in China for return cargoes of European goods. Return cargoes to China in junks usually comprised rice exports from Indo-China and Siam (Thailand).

Unscrupulous Chinese, Malays and Dyaks from Borneo soon realised what valuable objectives European ships provided in distant lonely waters, particularly around the spice islands of Indonesia. Throughout much of the 17th century and well into the 19th there must have been few coastal villages in the East Indies without their quota of thieves. Operating from armed prahus they played havoc with small ships in the coastal trade, but even worse were the locust-like attacks on East Indiamen unfortunate enough to be wrecked. In the early days the Dutch were the chief

sufferers, but as other Europeans expanded their eastern
trade they suffered equally. Any survivors were at risk of
becoming slaves, and wrecks were stripped bare. Some survivors who were at least able to get ashore might starve
because they could not salvage any food. Even men-of-war
could suffer like merchantmen in the Far East; the loss of
the frigate *Alceste,* Captain Murray Maxwell, R.N., in 1816,
is a case in point. She struck an uncharted rock near the
Philippines three miles off a small desolate island where,
eventually, all the 250 in the ship's company landed safely.
Soon the sea around was full of prahus with armed men who
rapidly stripped the wreck, from which a small guard had a
narrow escape, and then threatened those ashore after
burning the ship. With the few serviceable small-arms
available the attackers were kept away; equally serious was
the acute food shortage. Within a few days the island was
surrounded by over 600 men awaiting a chance to make a
landing, so it was practically impossible to send a ship's
boat to obtain help. The position became so grave that the
only hope of survival was the chance that *Alceste's* cutter
might fight her way through the blockade. Fortunately at
this critical juncture a British East Indiaman hove in sight,
at which the pirates scattered and everyone was rescued
safely. There was special comment at the time about the
extreme ferocity of the Malays in attempts they made to
land. One had been shot through the body, and while being
rescued by the British from the sea he seized a cutlass and
tried to wound his rescuers only a minute or so before he
died. In 1766, during his voyage round the world, the
celebrated Captain Cartaret in H.M.S. *Swallow* was attacked
off Mindanao in the Philippines. Despite most of the crew
being sick with scurvy and other incapacitating illnesses, the
attackers of *Swallow* were successfully beaten off and their
ship sunk. It was known at the time that this pirate had no
less than 30 ships in commission; the one involved in this
incident was armed with swivel-guns and small-arms. The
most notorious Chinese at the time were named Chinapoo
and Shap'ngtzai, and it is may well have been one of
their ships which attacked *Swallow*. Unfortunately, the

contemporary account does not specify whether the ship was a junk or an European-style vessel. That the ship, whatever her kind, was well armed is not surprising; actually junks were armed with cannons long before it was done in ships elsewhere in the world. The incident reveals how bold the Chinese must have been in their attacks on foreign ships, even if on this occasion, to their cost, the real nature of their opponent was misjudged; *Swallow,* a sloop, would at night resemble an East Indiaman.[5] The fate of any Europeans unfortunate enough to be taken prisoner was grim. They were mostly sold as slaves to the various potentates in Indo-China. Few escaped to tell the tale, while a failed escape involved death by Oriental torture at its worst. However intransigent responsible Chinamen may have been towards Europeans, at least they did not countenance slavery in their own country.

It is quite remarkable how the Chinese in junks were able successfully to attack European-style ships. This was done when the latter were becalmed; junks were able to progress or manoeuvre by using sweeps like the Algerian corsairs. Attacks of this kind went on well into the 19th century, when many merchantmen disappeared without trace. Some of these were undoubtedly lost on the uncharted reefs with which eastern seas abound; indeed, many known reefs are now named on charts by those various ships wrecked on them. But many missing ships fell to pirates, and the only trace of them revealed was, possibly a year or more after their disappearance, when an identifiable instrument or item of equipment might be offered for sale in a back street in Hong Kong or Canton. Cantonese pirate intelligence agents in Hong Kong would report the sailings of potential prizes from Hong Kong, so that they could be intercepted while still in local waters and even be attacked almost within sight of Hong Kong island.

The early direct formal European trade with China was at best a frustrating business because of the innate antipathy of the Chinese to Westerners. Later, things became easier when the demand for opium commenced, though the Chinese attitude remained basically that commerce involving ordinary

European trade goods was only useful insofar as it eased their own people of their superfluities and helped procure their necessities of life. China regarded itself as self-sufficient, and the influential ruling scholar-gentry were not interested in trading for trading's sake. An important consequence of this attitude was that the early European Charter Companies had to pay cash, usually silver, for the silk, porcelain and tea they wanted. Any private traders had to do similarly and carry ready money in their ships, which were more vulnerable to attack than those of the usually better and more heavily armed ships of the charter companies.

Silver was not always acceptable to the Chinese because the government maintained a careful balance between the amount of silver and gold and even copper in ordinary circulation; a measure easily administered by its highly efficient, albeit bureaucratic, civil service. Actually the first banknotes were issued in China to make the conveyance of money easier over long distances. The large cash payments which had to be made eroded the finances of the East India Company; so to balance the accounts towards the end of the 17th century they began shipping opium from India to China where the people rapidly acquired a taste for it, payment being cash or by barter for the goods increasingly demanded in the western world. I have a long-case clock bought by an ancestor in 1670; the front oak door is one of many of its kind made in England and sent specially to China to be lacquered. Was it paid for with opium? The Chinese finally reacted in 1729 by forbidding the importation of opium, but it was too late. This prohibition started the huge smuggling operations in which everyone connected with the sea participated, and Chinese piracy began in earnest, mainly to steal opium which could be disposed of so readily. It is remarkable to reflect now on the way the East India Company stepped up Indian opium production simply to meet the demands from smugglers and other questionable characters, who made such profits that to lose an occasional cargo (in ships belonging to other people) off the China coast was not a serious setback. Soon after the opium traffic started several million pounds' worth was being exported annually from India into China, a trade the Chinese could not stop owing to the long coastline. The Company originally established a fort in Canton in 1715, but had endless trouble there with Chinese bureaucracy, a state of affairs which did not improve until the important visit to Canton by Commodore Anson in 1741, during his voyage round the world. To prevent further difficulties with the Chinese the Company avoided carrying opium in its regularly chartered ships, and arranged with private individuals to do so. Special ships called wallahs were built in the East for the profitable trade; their European officers could soon make a pile if they escaped capture. Many wallahs were successfully attacked by pirates, as these ships were not fast sailers and their lascar crews not much good at fighting. By the end of the 18th century the opium traffic had become so big that special fast ships, the opium clippers, were built locally to permit two, and even three, round voyages annually to China from India, whereas the ordinary merchantmen used previously could only make one voyage a year, being dependent upon the monsoon winds. These new ships, like the others, were privately owned, and when successful, made large fortunes for their owners; men who needed money for a perfectly respectable venture in the United Kingdom would even spend a few years in the East simply to get the necessary. Most of the clippers hardly bothered about general cargo; it was opium outward-bound and the cash paid for it homeward-bound to a port in the Indian Ocean. These ships provided a better target for piracy than the ordinary East Indiaman trader because, despite being well armed and having European officers, there was always uncertainty whether lascar crews would actually defend an attacked ship. Any ship fortunate enough to carry a mainly European crew was much more likely to beat off attackers, the more so if, as was often the case, there were any British or United States naval deserters on board. Probably because of the basically unsavoury nature of the opium trade remarkably few details of much that went on are recorded.

The experiences of Mr. Jackson, a manager in the Far East for the Hong Kong and Shanghai Banking Corporation well over a hundred years ago, provide a further idea of what the local conditions used to be like, and are reproduced by courtesy of the Bank.[6]

'. . . Jackson had a curious personal connection with Singapore. His wife, whose maiden name was Amelia Dare, was captured by Singapore pirates in 1841 when she was a baby. Jackson married her in Yokohama while manager there in 1871. The story of how she escaped the pirates affords a glimpse of the Asian seas before the British navy had suppressed the pirates, a task not finally accomplished till the 20th century. At the end of December 1841 *Viscount Melbourne,* an East-Indiaman, while sailing from Singapore to Hong Kong, was wrecked on the Luconia shoal off Brunei in Borneo. The crew and passengers took to the boats and headed back for Singapore, 600 miles away. On the fourth day, when the Captain was reading Sunday prayers, what they feared was a pirate prahu bore down on them. An account survives of what happened, written by a junior officer of the *Viscount Melbourne.* He was ordered to take a small boat attached to the Captain's gig, meet the prahu and find out what it was. "When we got alongside we spoke, the boatswain acting as interpreter. They said that they came to conduct us safely inshore and that one boat was there already. By this we suspected that they had taken them prisoners and wished to entice the rest of us to the same fate. They now said that they wished to see the Captain, so we pulled back". The prahu followed and went alongside the Captain's gig, "where all were ready, cutlass in hand, to receive them in case of treachery. They tried all they could to persuade us to go with them and finally began to make fast the Captain's boat with a rattan rope. When they found that we could not go with them, they assumed a very threatening aspect; so that, there being so few of us who could fight and our firearms being useless on account of the preceding rain, the Captain gave orders to cut and run. The cook with his cutlass severed their rope and we all made sail!"

'The prahu chased them and opened fire, a ball from one of its cannon passing between the Captain and Mrs. Dare,

Thomas Jackson's future mother-in-law, who was on board with two infants. The other two boats kept ahead, but the Captain's gig was overtaken. When within a few fathoms they made signs to us to desist pulling, at the same time taking aim at us. The prahu was about the size of a sloop, neatly built of teak but cleverly camouflaged to look like any boat. She had two long straight poles for masts and a large lug made of matting to each. Besides this they pulled fifteen sweeps a side. When they first came alongside, there were only five or six fellows like fishermen visible on deck, but now her decks were crowded with Malays armed with krises, very dangerous crooked poisonous swords, clubs, spears and guns which gave them a ferocious appearance. They jumped into our boat, seized upon us and would, I think, have despatched us at once, had it not been for the interference of one who seemed their chief, who, dashing away the swords of the most forward, ordered all but two to get into their own craft and pursue the other boats which by this time were a good way ahead. The Malay chief then told the British to steer for the land (probably the coast of Sarawak) and was beginning to collect their belongings in a blanket, when the pirates of the prahu, instead of doing what they were told, got on to the gig again to share in the loot. They began to clear the gig of everything—clothes, provisions and even our drop of water, about two gallons, for the sake of the keg. They danced with joy at the sight of the muskets and pistols and, coming on the sextant, asked the writer to explain its use, which he did. When everything had been transferred to the prahu, the Captain begged the chief to let them rejoin the other boats, which by this time were nearly out of sight. Surprisingly to relate, he nodded his head assentingly and shook us by the hand. The Captain in his gratitude pulled a 50 rupee note and some silver from his pocket and handed them to the chief. This was a mistake, for the rest of the pirates began to strip us for more. They took the Captain's watch and whatever other watches and rings they found. Satisfied at last, they let the English go, with a parting present of a basket of sago and three pints of water. The Chief politely shook hands with us all and they, stepping aboard the prahu, made sail towards the shore. We made sail and, pulling at the same time with all our might, rejoined our comrades in the other boards.'

It was another eight days before they reached Singapore. They had had a narrow escape from death or enslavement.

In contrast to the usually satisfactory and even happy outcome of Wild West stories, in pirate stories the bad men usually got things all their own way; rarely was a pirate ship captured other than by men-of-war. One of the few instances when the situation was completely reversed occurred in 1793. Captain Woodard from Boston, Massachusetts, made a local voyage from Bombay to Manila as mate in an American ship, *Enterprise,* which, due to delays by bad weather, ran out of provisions. In the Macassa Straits his captain sent him to a ship they sighted to try and obtain some, but owing to further deterioration in the weather he failed to regain his own ship.

For nearly two years during attempts to reach Macassa, Woodard and his companions remained the prisoners of various Malay communities. They were finally held, apparently for good, at a place called Tombon which was about 200 miles from their objective. One day in came a pirate vessel which had a fine sea-going canoe as a tender. Woodard and the four men with him somehow evaded their captors and seized the canoe in which they escaped. Their journey to Macassa was still not without further adventure, but the port was eventually reached, whence they all took ship to Bombay. Shortly after getting there Woodard's former captain in *Enterprise* arrived in a new ship from America. In Bombay, Captain Woodard was given command of another ship belonging to the same company.

Chinese pirates were active until well after World War I, usually operating from nooks and crannies mostly north of Hong Kong. Bias Bay, now called Taya Bay, is a name which always suggests piracy. A favourite method was to sign on in the crew of small locally trading merchantmen, then to seize the ship when somewhere near a place like Bias Bay. Another method was to embark as deck passengers on some local run and, at the appointed time and place, storm the bridge and overpower the officers. To stop this sort of happening in local steamers, many had the centre-castle and bridge section surrounded with stout steel netting to fence off aggressive passengers.

It was in the China seas, as in other parts of the globe, that British naval power put an end to most troubles of this sort, something from which all nations benefited. Now, however, the world situation is such that, with the regrettable decline in British naval power, even the British Chamber of Shipping believes that piracy may well start again in narrow waters and in other places where no one in recent years would have dared to contemplate such action for fear of the consequences. Whether the hi-jacking of aircraft will develop into the modern counterpart of conventional piracy is a matter of opinion.

Notes

1. *Les pirates à Madagascar en XVIIme et XVIIIme siècles.* Des Champs, Paris. 1949.
2. *The Madagascan Pirates.* Arnold Foster. New York. 1957.
3. *A Voyage to New Guinea and the Moluccas.* Thos. Forrest. London. 1779.
4. Cited by Foster (*loc. cit.*).
5. *The Polite Traveller.* Vol. VII. 1783.
6. *Wayfoong.* Maurice Collis. Faber and Faber. 1965.

CHAPTER VI

WHAT WERE THE PRIZES?

I

THE NATURE OF THE PRIZES to be obtained at any period largely depended upon the pattern of world trade; indeed, changes in trade influenced the actual manner in which piracy was conducted at particular times. Certain trade routes have always been notable for the high value of the goods passing along them. Obviously pirates knew the most favourable routes and planned accordingly. This explains the constant attacks, from time immemorial, made on ships not merely trading locally in the Eastern Mediterranean, and on other valuable cargoes often operating the final sea stage—across the Mediterranean—of the otherwise over-land Far East trade route from India and from China through the Middle East. Along it were carried such things as silks, spices, precious stones, and indigo, to the communities in Asia Minor and around the Mediterranean littoral. In addition to this overland route, many of the commodities originating in India and even in the Far East desired by these communities were conveyed by sea, with its attendant hazards; so it was little wonder many merchantmen carried archers for defence.

As explained in Chapter II there existed for so long the vast seaborne trade of the early Levantine mariners and the Phoenicians. The immense amount of gold brought from Ophir alone must have attracted thieves, just as happens nowadays when gold is moved about. Shipments of several hundred talents at a time appear to have been quite usual, and since a talent was about £20,000 of our money, simple arithmetic indicates the value of such cargoes. Exactly where Ophir was situated is uncertain; some believe it to have been in Southern Arabia, others in Somaliland; but it was most likely the place conveniently near the source of South African gold now known as Sofala in Mozambique. Here traces of early Egyptian contacts still exist and it is considered by some authorities to be the Punt to which treasure-seeking voyages were made by the Egyptians on various occasions, presumably in ships chartered from the Levant. The first recorded voyage to Punt was made *c*. B.C. 3000 during the Sahu-Rê dynasty. Wherever it was situated Ophir was well known by B.C. 1500, and for centuries was the major source of gold for the civilised world.[1] In addition to gold and ivory there was sustained demand for the valuable manganese ore pyrolusite in Egypt, the Middle East and India, where it was used as a variously-coloured glaze for pottery, glass and kindred manufactures. This ore was mined in what is now Rhodesia, whence it was shipped in large quantities. Professor Dart and others, by local research, have demonstrated that this important trade started about B.C. 4000 and probably lasted until about B.C. 1000.[2]

Throughout recorded history jewels have played an important part in the life of mankind, both for adornment and for their intrinsic value. All the precious stones of today were known to the ancients, but there was always particular emphasis on rubies and pearls to symbolise anything of great value. Among the many references to rubies probably the most expressive is the way they are mentioned in the charming story in Proverbs (31, 1) about the advice to King Lemuel by his mother. There are many equally understandable symbolic uses of pearls; in fact, they were chosen by Our Lord in His parable about the Palestinian pearl merchant (Matt. 13, 45).

More than any other nation the Romans appreciated pearls, and the demand for them by their women actually imposed a drain on the national resources. The Indians, who were the chief suppliers, would not readily accept Mediterranean goods in exchange. They required payment in gold for jewels and their other important export, pepper, which was also in great demand by the Romans, just as other European nations wanted it later on. Pliny, writing about A.D. 70 in *Historia Naturalis,* refers to the extravagances of Roman women and the effect these extravagances had on what would now be called the balance of payments. In consequence ships outward-bound in the Indian trade always had large amounts of specie on board for their cash purchases, and returned with equally valuable cargoes; little wonder they were so often attacked by Arab pirates, particularly around the Gulf of Aden where the coast was so suitable for lairs.

It is interesting to speculate whether pirates in those days who captured a supply of rubies or other gems carried some as pocket money, in the manner that New World pirates would use emeralds for spending money in brothels. But these Arabs were, so to speak, local men operating in their own part of the world, with domestic ties in the many shore settlements then existing. After Europeans started trading with India by the long sea route via the Cape there was a sudden upsurge in the export of diamonds from the Coromandel Coast in the Bay of Bengal. This trade was short-lived, not only because of access difficulties, but also because of the risks of theft while transporting the gems in small boats to ships waiting offshore.

From its inception the world spice and aromatic trade was remarkable for its magnitude and value. It was started by the Pharaohs to satisfy the Egyptian need for raw materials to manufacture incense, the use of which became the recognised token of respect. With such an original use in heathen temples it came to be part of public and domestic ceremonial, a practice continuing to this day, though it is now only used for ecclesiastical purposes. To save imports from afar, spices and various aromatic herbs gradually came to be grown in the Middle East; but always the main sources of them were India, Ceylon and the Far East. Mauritius was the original source of cloves, which were only introduced into Zanzibar 150 years ago to make it the chief source of supply nowadays. That a distant island like Mauritius in the Indian Ocean could be regularly located and reached several thousand years ago provides a striking instance of the skills possessed by the ancient navigators. Herodotus (II and IV) remarks how the Egyptians obtained cinnamon from India, a source he thought dated from the time when one of the Pharaohs named Sosostris (there were three Pharaohs of that name in succession at one period) overran the Indian sub-continent many centuries earlier. He describes how this Pharaoh erected pillars at the limits of his conquests inscribed 'Sosostris, king of kings, and lord of lords, subdued this country by the power of his arms.' A few of these monuments survived until the time of Herodotus, one of which stood in Further India.

It could be a comment on all the foregoing that for several thousand years the ships on the main trade routes of the world were carrying specialist cargoes almost comparable in value to those in the Spanish treasure ships of comparatively recent times, and were attacked by pirates at every opportunity.

Another spice, cardamom, used as early as B.C. 1500, and still used both in food and medicine, later became a favourite with the Norsemen during the time they had settlements in Spain and North Africa. Later with the expansion of the Ottoman Empire there must have been plenty of ships with spice cargoes in and around the Dardanelles, because the Turks for a time nearly monopolised the European spice trade. The overland trade routes to the Far East practically ceased after the Turks captured Constantinople in 1453, which stimulated the opening up of the Cape route to the Far East, with new hazards.

As civilisation and standards of living in Western European countries improved there was still further demand for Eastern spices, chiefly to render more palatable the unpalatable and often tainted food of those days. It was a sudden increase in the London price of pepper at the end of the 16th century which led to the founding of the English East India Company. By then, in their turn, the Dutch had cornered the spice trade; pepper they bought overseas could show a profit of 1,000 per cent. by the time it was sold in Europe. How tempting it must have been to obtain a spice cargo on the high seas for nothing with the knowledge it could be disposed of so easily.

When there might not be much doing at sea in the Mediterranean, pirates often made raids ashore. Thucydides (1 : 7) pointed out how inhabited sites, in early days both on islands and on the mainland, were some distance inland, a practice lasting, in fact, until early last century. Right up until the 16th century, all Mediterranean navigation ceased after the Feast of Atonement (10 October) with the onset of wintry weather. But the time came when ships from Northern Europe could remain at sea all the year round and were attracted to the Mediterranean in the winter to pick up anything of value to be found ashore or afloat; in this they were well rewarded, because of the seaworthiness of the vessels and the skill of their crews. The principal sufferers were the Genoese merchants, who complained bitterly about their losses. In the *Merchant of Venice* (I, iii), Shakespeare makes contemporary reference to what was happening '. . . An argosy bound to Tripoli, another to the Indies . . . a third to Mexico, a fourth for England . . . But ships are but boards, sailors, but men: there be land-rates and water-rates, water-thieves and land-thieves, I mean pirates . . .'

II

In the Narrow Seas, as northern European waters used to be called, trade was slow in starting, apart from the rather specialised export from the British Isles to the Mediterranean of tin, copper, and later, in Roman times, lead. For many centuries England and Spain were the principal sources of non-ferrous metals for Europe, sources originally believed to have been discovered by the Phoenicians who made regular voyages to fetch cargoes in exchange for wines and domestic luxury goods. An interesting local tradition exists in the Quantocks (Somerset) that the whortleberries, which grow there in such profusion, were wanted by the Phoenicians for the preparation of the renowned Tyrian purple dye. This dye was normally obtained from *murex trunculus,* a

shellfish of the Eastern Mediterranean. Still, there are sugges-
tions that the mollusc became increasingly scarce as a result
of the continuous demand for it, thus explaining the
latter-day, albeit traditional, use of Somerset whortleberries from which an excellent purple dye can be
prepared. To help this scarcity of *murex trunculus* a
regular traffic was started *c.* B.C. 800 from the Levant
to the Canary Islands to obtain a special lichen for use
in dyeing.

Among the early prizes to be had in northern waters was
the Roman silver currency used in England, practically the
only country in the Empire in which silver coins were in
circulation after A.D. 360.[3] The numerous large hoards of
late-dated silver coins (and sometimes other treasures, too)
discovered over the centuries in the West of England is
remarkable; few similar have been unearthed elsewhere.
Most coins are dated towards the end of the Roman occupation and all appear to have been hidden in a manner suggestive
of some emergency. It is believed that Irish pirates became
active about the time Roman troops were withdrawn from
England, and Dr. Haverfield, a distinguished archaeologist,
suggested many years ago that the money may have been
hidden from these pirates. It is significant that at Coleraine
in Northern Ireland a large hoard of silver coins of contemporary dates, together with silver ingots, has been discovered,
obviously related to the use of silver coinage in England
then.[4] The coins were mostly minted in Continental Europe,
and since the Romans never occupied Ireland there was no
reason for their silver coins being there other than as the
result of some irregularity.

Large-scale piracy by the Norsemen was actively carried
on independently from their invasions of various European
countries, though a Norseman anywhere could be regarded
as a potential pirate. Their chief ravages were directed against
the early cities and towns in Northern Europe, and since
most urban riches were in the hands of the Church any
accessible monasteries were favourite and easy targets for
raids. Around the coasts of the British Isles, France and
Spain, the Norsemen came and went as they pleased; in

A.D. 845 they even went up the Seine and occupied Paris, only leaving when they were paid 1,400 marks.

Later on, when the Normans became so progressive and enterprising, including their successful invasion of England in 1066, general commerce in north-western Europe expanded rapidly and soon attracted thieves of all nationalities. The European demand for wool, chiefly produced in England, was the principal factor in the growing prosperity of this country, in fact, the export trade became so large that much had to be carried in foreign bottoms. English shipping expanded to handle the traffic and this resulted in even more piracy. So bad did it become that in the reign of Edward III (1327–1377) special ships were detailed to keep the English Channel clear. For a number of years this was done successfully, but eventually control lapsed and Channel piracy became an accepted thing. A couple of hundred years later Elizabeth I also tried to do something about policing the Channel by posting men to what was then the uninhabited island of Sark. These were the forefathers of some of the islanders today.

As the export of raw wool from England declined it was replaced by a much larger and more profitable export of cloth. For pirates it was something really good, since it was easier to dispose of valuable bolts of cloth than bales of wool. An unusual export at this time was firewood, to provide fuel for the treeless parts of Northern Europe before coal-mining started there. Whether cargoes of firewood were ever seized must remain problematical, but they must have been of value. The chief imports by sea to this country were domestic luxury goods such as wine, oil, soap and fruit, though canvas and salt are frequently mentioned in old cargo manifests. In late Tudor and early Stuart times timber was a very important and valuable export from Southern Ireland, which was the chief source of the oak needed in Spain for manufacturing the large wine casks called pipes. A colleague whose ancestors had always lived near Cork (Corcaigh) once explained to me what close ties used to exist with Spain, from which wines and domestic commodities were sent in exchange for pipe staves of which many thousands were exported annually. Unfortunately, pirates of various nationalities knew how saleable these staves were on the Continent.

In Scandinavia, when Peter the Great, around 1700, was doing so much to modernise Russia and to open up foreign trade through the Baltic, the temptations to the unscrupulous became substantial. That was the time a particularly unpleasant Dane named Derdrake, about whom more will be said later, specialised in stealing arms, ships' fittings, and woollen goods consigned to Russia. He found a ready market for these in Sweden until he was dealt with.

Right up to the end of the 16th century any merchantman peacefully trading in the Channel and its approaches was liable to attack by all and sundry: Englishmen on their part freely attacked Flemings and Frenchmen. However, by the end of that century the amount of jewels and specie to be won from Spanish vessels actually made the New World the most profitable sphere of operations for everybody.

This important change in practice did not affect the corsairs based on Algiers and adjacent North African harbours. Apart from a few intermissions resulting from punitive attacks by European Powers in attempts to restrain their activities, the corsairs continued to harass shipping off the Iberian Peninsula and in the Western Approaches from the mid-16th century until about 1800. Keen as they were to seize cargoes, they were equally keen to seize European crews or passengers for slavery.

These slaves either had to work in Algerian ships, which could have as many as 200 on board, working under the notoriously cruel galley masters, or else they were sent into the hinterland of North Africa to the various Arab and Moorish rulers for use at their pleasure. Few of those who suffered in this manner were heard of again. Occassionally a well-known or wealthy person captured might be held for a substantial ransom, of the order of 6,000 dollars, but few were so fortunate. One of the fortunates was Jean Vaillant, a contemporary of Colbert the Frenchman who introduced Letters of Marque for privateers in the time

of Louis XIV. Vaillant was a physician, but also was a
recognised authority on medals, about which he advised the
king for the royal collection. With Colbert's assistance,
Vaillant made several journeys to Persia and other Middle
East countries to obtain rare specimens. While returning
from one of these missions his ship was captured by a corsair
and he was held prisoner in Algiers for five months. Eventually he was ransomed and allowed to retain 20 of the gold
medals he had collected. The ship in which he was travelling
back to Marseilles was attacked by yet another corsair,
and to prevent the medals being found in his possession
he swallowed the lot. A timely shift of wind saved the ship
from capture and the mouth of the Rhône was reached
safely, where Vaillant got ashore in a small boat, thoroughly
uncomfortable, with about 300 grammes of gold inside him.
This, as was remarked at the time, did not pass through as
readily as a dose of salts. The doctors in the South of France
tried to advise about the somewhat unusual complaint of
their colleague, but nature relieved him of most of the
treasure in his inside by the time he arrived in Lyons. There
he awaited the remaining medals which were expected daily,
including one of great rarity and value. All were duly voided,
much to the satisfaction of Louis XIV, whose favour Vaillant
retained until his death at the age of seventy-four.

The actual number of Europeans made slaves is unknown,
but it must have been very large. To give an idea of the number readily available for some special toil: Hayradin, a king of
Algiers in the 16th century, had 30,000 continually at work
for three years building the harbour Mole. Even soldiers
taken prisoner were made slaves. When Charles V of Spain
attacked the city in 1541, his large army met with disaster
in a storm and there were so many prisoners to be sold that
the market was glutted, and many men 'only fetched an
onion apiece'. After one quite small naval engagement with
Venetian ships as many as 1,500 galley slaves were rescued
by the victors.

Europeans of all nationalities were captured for slavery,
more particularly the Spanish, and, somewhat later, the
French—both peoples always busily trading in and around

the Straits of Gibraltar and adjacent waters. The south coast
of France was often raided, too. Early in the 17th century,
when the Moors were expelled from Spain, they reinforced
the existing Arab-Algerian piracy to make it sufficiently
notorious for the Ottoman government to issue a rebuke,
which evoked a reply that 'their depredations deserved to
be indulged to them, seeing that they were the only bulwark
against the Spaniards, the sworn enemies of the Moslem
name. If they should pay a punctilious regard to all that
could purchase peace or liberty to trade with the Ottoman
Empire, they would have nothing to do but set fire to all
their shipping, and turn camel drivers for a livelihood'.[5]

With the Moorish reinforcements the corsairs became even
bolder in their search for slaves, and, apart from people taken
from ships, there were various shore raids around Naples and
also in the Adriatic. After any semblance of Turkish influence
was renounced in 1623, the corsairs, spreading out into the
Atlantic, soon made shore raids on Ireland for prisoners.
Later, about 1630, when operating in the Bristol Channel,
they actually landed north of where Weston-super-Mare
now stands and carried off the men and women from a
nearby village. In time they reached as far north as Iceland,
and, on one occasion, captured 500 of the islanders, an event
made possible by help from a renegade seaman who had been
taken prisoner earlier in a Danish ship. From all this it can
be seen that seeking slaves was far from an activity only
involving negroes from the Guinea coast of Africa.

The corsairs used a special kind of vessel, but having no
suitable material of their own from which to build them,
the materials from captured ships were utilised.

III

Although immense prizes were to be won in the New
World the tendency is to highlight such successes. Successes
in any walk of life are talked about, not the less notable
events or failures; and failures there were. Many who thought
piracy was a certain path to riches discovered to their cost
how true was the remark in a book published at the time by

the Dutchman Esquemeling, that pieces of eight do not
grow on every tree.[6]

In the early days of the New World there is frequent
mention of pieces of eight. A piece of eight was a silver coin
worth at that time about 25p., but much more today. It
got its name because it was an eight-reales piece (half a
Spanish peseta) which had an '8' on one side and an 'R' on
the other. Twelve-and-a-half pieces of eight was the value
of a dubloon, a gold coin naturally more sought-after. The
modern sign $ is derived from the $ sign used by pirates
to signify the eight-reales coin, which itself may be regarded
as the forerunner of the existing dollar monetary system.
This provides a further example of how ruffians left their
mark on world history.

Spanish ships remained the greatest attraction for so long
because of the treasure they carried to Europe. There is no
modern parallel to the booty, mostly gold, taken by the
conquerors of South America; almost the sole objective of
Spanish expeditions there was gold. Just one single haul from
the Peruvians amounted to three-and-a-half million pounds
sterling, and there were others approaching this figure. Had
the English, the French, or the Dutch turned south instead
of concentrating on North America how different might have
been the ultimate result.[7]

Gold and silver taken directly from the Incas and others
were not the only sources of treasure. As colonisation
proceeded, precious metal mines were put into regular
production in Peru, while deposits of gems, particularly
emeralds, were developed and worked by European methods.
Pearl fishing in the Rio del Hacha was also started. Where
did all these vast riches finish up? No one really knows.

During Drake's piratical expedition to the West Indies in
1585 he had an unusual, but apparently very welcome,
prize when taking a Spanish ship near Ushant. She had a
large cargo of excellent fresh salt fish which Drake distributed through his fleet in which were no less than 2,500
men. Afterwards further additions were made to his victuals
in Vigo, which he occupied especially to rescue a number of
Englishmen imprisoned there. He then visited Santiago in

the Cape de Verde islands where some Plymouth sailors had recently been murdered. He stripped the place bare and proceeded to the New World where he was only moderately successful, due mainly to the ravages of yellow fever; finally only 700 of his men remained fit for duty. Things of a domestic character often taken from Spanish ships were the stone jars used for wine and to supplement the water supplies normally contained in barrels, where it rapidly deteriorated. These jars were also found to be useful overseas as a means of carrying fresh water from a spring or stream some distance from a beach.

When local opposition at sea in the New World happened for a while to be too strong, or prizes were not very plentiful, pirates successfully attacked towns and settlements ashore. If it were considered that sufficient loot was not readily found, then a town would be held to ransom. Vera Cruz in Mexico, the first place treated in this fashion by the buccaneers, produced £437,500; half of this sum was forthcoming in a single day. In 1697 a direct attack on Carthagena in Columbia produced £1,750,000. At about the same time a Jamaican, named John Davis, took only 80 men in three canoes up river into Nicaragua, a journey lasting a week. He returned with $50,000 worth of general booty and 4,000 pieces of eight.

As colonisation of the New World expanded, a profitable venture was to attack outward-bound merchantmen, often sailing alone, which carried large general cargoes for the European settlers in the Americas. These stolen cargoes were sold to colonists, as it were in the ordinary course of business, but, of course, at substantial profit. Something in constant demand overseas was European clothing. It is only in the present century that folk living in the tropics have dressed for the climate; more or less ordinary-style clothing was worn previously, a practice concerning which Sir Hans Sloane, the physician, commented upon unfavourably while in Jamaica in 1688. In those days we note that an item such as a reconditioned beaver hat could fetch as much as $20. For long periods many Spanish coastal settlements were entirely dependent on domestic goods only obtainable from pirates, who sometimes gained complete control of local interport shipping routes; a remarkable situation.

Long before Sir Walter Raleigh introduced tobacco into England the Spaniards had learnt all about it from the Indians of Central America. Ashore, cigars became very popular with the European colonists, whereas seafarers mostly smoked pipes, possibly because of their convenience and the lessened fire risk. It was soon realised that, just like today, there was good tobacco and bad tobacco, and quite a large trade in it developed locally between the Darien Isthmus, where it was then mainly produced, and the new cities and towns springing up. When European pirates got busy in this region a consignment of good tobacco was a welcome prize, which not only could they use themselves, but sell at a good profit for ultimate transmission to Europe. Another domestic commodity increasingly valuable was sugar, once its popularity in Europe was established (there was little sugar used in England before the Stuart period).

Something else which rapidly became valuable resulted from the most important medical discovery in the late 16th century: that extracts of Peruvian bark, of which the active principle is quinine, provided a specific treatment for malaria, or ague, as the disease used to be called. Ague was a disease not then peculiar to the tropics, being common in Europe and elsewhere. The bark treatment, long used by the local inhabitants of the tropical New World, was rapidly adopted by Europeans, not only there, but in other malarious regions whenever supplies of this remarkable medicine could be obtained. The demand for Peruvian bark, or Jesuits' bark, soon greatly exceeded readily available supplies, mainly because the Indians who collected it in the forests became increasingly reluctant to help the colonial Spaniards any more than they were obliged. Pirates needed quinine like everybody else and obtained supplies wherever they could, selling the surplus. When Captain Sharp was operating along the west coast of South America he made a number of shore raids; during a raid on Arica in 1687 he found a house stuffed full of the bark, an unusual but very valuable haul. However, there must have been some who did not yet realise the great importance and value of the bark. There was a German surgeon named Dr. Fritz practising in Port Royal, Jamaica, who at one time had sailed with the renowned Captain Townley in the Pacific in the mid 17th century. He told Sir Hans Sloane, already mentioned, how they had taken a Spanish ship, *Cafcarilla,* with a cargo of bark which was thrown overboard to make room for sea stores before the ship was taken into pirate service.

Pirates, in the New World as everywhere else, always liked loot to be easy to handle, so the valuable cargo in an ordinary homeward-bound merchantman would, from their point of view, be regarded as almost worthless unless there were receivers about willing to do a deal. Any cash or valuables of consequence in the ordinary American trader were more likely to be found on board when outward-bound. Cash was needed to buy African slaves, and the proceeds of the sale in the New World was often used to buy a cargo for home. A typical homeward manifest:

> 26 hogsheads, 3 tierces,[8] and 3 barrels of rum
> 25 hogsheads of molasses
> 3 barrels, 3 tierces of sugar
> 2 packets of cotton
> 60 weights of indigo
> oddments

Anything at all bulky tended to be ignored, partly through failure to realise how valuable bulky cargoes sometimes were. One of these was logwood (*Heamatoxylon campeachianeum*) constantly needed in Europe for dyeing. Logwood was chiefly obtained around the Gulf of Campeachy; there it cost as much as £3 a ton, so was much more valuable by the time it reached Europe. Large quantities were burnt by those unaware of its real value simply to get rid of it, or else it was used as ready-cut firewood. One Spanish ship, captured intact with a full cargo, was sailed to England, yet only on arrival did her new captain discover that he had treasure of an unexpected sort in the hold of his prize.

IV

The ships of all nations trading in Eastern or Far Eastern waters were always at risk, more particularly after the Cape route was opened up, when there was a great increase in the number of small vessels used by local traders. Then, very much like today, small ships poked in and out of small ports and obscure anchorages around the Indian Ocean and the Eastern Archipelago, to pick up parcels of such things as spices for transhipment at convenient places into the larger European East Indiamen.

The small coasters, which usually had native crews, were easy to attack; but as trade increased many of these coasters came to be owned and commanded by European seamen who had settled in the Far East. With better crews and armament these coasters became tougher targets; nevertheless, many fell victim and their crews were either killed or put ashore to be made slaves in Indo-China. The favourite time for attacking these ships was when they were anchored in some out-of-the-way place, or becalmed, as happened in the Mediterranean. The attackers swarmed on board from piraguas emerging from the many sheltered inlets with which eastern seas abound. Dampier, the famous navigator, who had intimate knowledge of the East Indies, refers to several events of this kind in his books describing his experiences in that region.

The cargoes of outward-bound East Indiamen consisted of ordinary trade goods for India and the Far East, together with bulk supplies to meet the domestic needs of expatriate Europeans. Homeward-bound, the cargoes comprised such things as silk, tea, spices and Indian cotton piece-goods, all valuable commodities (tea sold at anything between 25p and 50p a pound in Europe), but such things were bulky. These bulky stolen cargoes were often bought by unscrupulous dealers who would send ships specially to pick them up, to be sold later in Europe, or, frequently, along the Atlantic seaboard of the New World.

As the usual practice everywhere was to burn captured ships after they had been pillaged, many a good ship was burnt after being stripped of anything in the way of jewels, specie, or easily-transported valuables. Some cargoes must have been examined and appraised very carelessly; still, the men doing this were hardly experienced stevedores. One ship, actually in the Caribbean, was sent to the bottom in disgust because her hold was thought to contain merely a cargo of iron bars, whereas these bars were silver ingots. The mistake was discovered too late.

How the demand for slaves by the Arab rulers in North Africa was met by the corsairs has already been described but in the seas around Arabia an immense slave trade existed for centuries to meet requirements in the Middle East. African negroes were supplied in large numbers and the Red Sea slave trade, in which the Arabs ultimately obtained a monopoly, continued long after this unsavoury business ceased elsewhere in the world. It was finally suppressed by the Royal Navy less than a hundred years ago. Slaves with fair skins, when obtainable, were always preferred to negroes, but the supply was limited either to any Europeans unfortunate enough to be captured at sea, or fair-skinned people from parts of the Indian sub-continent and around the Persian Gulf. Since all generations of pirates were interested in anything that could be turned into money, cargoes of slaves did not escape their attentions. The first authentic instance of which I know occurred in the 18th century when an European pirate, working the Indian Ocean, seized a cargo of Asian women. Just where these women originated or where they were destined is unknown: what is known is that their captor's ship was wrecked on the island of Bourbon, now called Réunion. The French had already started to colonise this fertile island to grow various food-stuffs, thereby making the place a popular call for ships in the Eastern trade needing stores. The island also established a reputation among sailors as a good source of women, and the unexpected additional supply appears to have been greatly welcomed.

A good many years later another cargo of slaves was captured on its way to the West Indies by a well-known man, Bartholomew Jones, who was a former English sea officer. He had fitted out an unlicensed privateer after leaving the Navy, but because the ship had no proper Letter of Marque he initially got into endless trouble. On this occasion he was only able to sell the negroes to a Jew in Jamaica for a cut price of £25 each. However, in course of time he was more successful and was able to retire a rich man.

V

The special form that piracy took in the Far East and the China Seas, which mainly concerned the opium traffic, has already been described in Chapter V.

As piracy spread in the Malay Archipelago and the China Seas the risks involved in conveying much money by sea became increasingly hazardous. This led to the introduction of a central banking system in the East long before much was done about it in the Western world. The system was based on book entries rather resembling banking methods used all over the world nowadays. Very large sums were turned over by the early Far East merchants, and inevitably a lot of cash had to be carried in merchantmen, particularly in the China trade, where so much business was transacted on a cash-and-carry basis. The *Grosvenor*, an East Indiaman, wrecked on the South African coast in 1782, had about two million pounds on board and at this very moment attempts are being made to locate the wreck. To avoid the attendant risks of sending too much cash about in ships, merchants often arranged to make debits and credits against each other; they would also do this sort of thing on commission for private individuals and the smaller traders. Ultimately, merchants' consortiums formed the basis of the special banks now operating in the Far East.

This problem of how to transmit large sums of money and valuables, collectively called treasure, safely across the seas must have troubled men from the beginning of sea trade. Treasure was always at risk, either from pirates waiting to pounce, or from hostile men-of-war. When regular English naval vessels came into use, it was realised that the safest way to convey treasure was in King's ships, as they were originally called. At one time the captain of any ship, whether a King's ship or a merchantman, was the man who really decided what he would carry in the ship under his command. For a consideration he was usually willing to convey privately-owned treasure. The consideration for the service rendered became known as freight money, particularly in the navy, where it remained a captain's perquisite until early this century. Because of the money involved in the Oriental trades the captain of any naval ship ordered to or from the East was fairly certain to be asked by the East India Company, or one of the large merchant houses, to convey treasure for them. The usual commission, or freight money, was 2½ per cent.; this added up if possibly half a million pounds was involved. On local runs in the Far East in areas of risk, private deals by captains for services rendered were made on the spot.

An old Chinese hand I met in Hong Kong many years ago, when talking about pirates, explained that though they wanted cargoes of opium or anything else of value there was something they wanted nearly as much. This was rope and cordage of any description, which was avidly taken for eventual use in the thousands of junks around the China coast. Even in the present century the chief officer of any ship takes great care not to leave rope lying about, as it simply disappears.

Notes

1. *Peake's Commentary on the Bible.* 1962 edn.
2. *South African Archaeological Bulletin*, 8, 91. Raymond A. Dart. December 1953.
3. *Monsen-Blocas*, III, 133.
4. *Victoria History of the Counties of England*, vol. I. 1902.
5. *Encyclopaedia Britannica*. 1797.
6. *The Buccaneers of America.* Esquemeling. Swan Sonnenschein edn. 1893.
7. *Prescott's Conquest of Peru.* Original edn. 1847.
8. A large barrel mainly used at the time for American exports of tallow (about 400lbs.).

CHAPTER VII

RECRUITMENT

THE ANSWER TO THE QUESTION as to how men became pirates is not entirely given by the old saying that opportunity makes the thief; though inducements for robbery have always been as great, if not greater, at sea than on land. Recruiting Europeans for piracy in home waters must always have been easy; there were plenty of shore bases and voyages were not prolonged. Then as piracy spread overseas the large prizes to be won attracted plenty of recruits to a life mainly spent in the tropics, though possible death from one of the local diseases was an added risk to a risky life.

Without in any way justifying what happened, it must be appreciated that there were occasions when events over which sailors had no control forced them into piracy in a big way. A curious economic situation once involved some Englishmen; an event which arose thiswise. Until the period of Reformation, English fishermen used to provide much of the fish required on Fridays by Roman Catholics in Northern Europe. Chester men customarily fished the Irish Sea, while the English Iceland fishery supplied Normandy and Brittany as well as much of England. With the Reformation a large market was suddenly lost and men were thrown out of work, despite various Acts of Parliament to encourage greater consumption of fish. These must have constituted an early version of the 'Eat More Fish' campaigns to boost sales, of the kind with which we are all familiar. Out-of-work fishermen, who were highly skilled seamen, took the easy, and almost only, way to mitigate their hardships.

Much later on in Tudor times, when robbing Spaniards at sea (and on land) became practically a national duty, this was not regarded as piracy by Englishmen, who were always ready to have a go at the Spaniards who wanted to dominate the world. The English attitude to Spain was much as it was four hundred years later when Germany tried to do the same sort of thing. However, we must accept the fact that Drake, John Hawkins, and others of our national heroes were pirates for at least part of their lives, though they would have denied this. Still there must have been 'tough'uns' in their crews who were out for what they could get, 'to go a-pyrating', or as it was expressed euphemistically rather later, 'to go on the account'. In 1593 when Richard Hawkins, son of John Hawkins, made his unsuccessful voyage to the Pacific, his commission makes it clear that the object was the usual one to loot from 'the King of Spain, his subjects and adherents'. After his ship *Dainty* was defeated and captured by a Spanish squadron off the coast of what is now Ecuador, Hawkins and his crew were very humanely treated by the Spaniards, which was very unusual at the time.

But, taking them as a whole, there is much to indicate that, particularly during the reign of Elizabeth I, many men regarded themselves as Crusaders against the Spaniards, with good material rewards to offset the risks incurred. For rather different reasons the French, the Portuguese, the Swedes, and, to a lesser extent, the Dutch, were just as eager to rob the Spaniards in the New World. The French, for a couple of centuries, were always ready to find the flimsiest excuse to attack the Spaniards. Because the Dutch possessed such prosperous fishing and whaling industries, and for a time more or less controlled the Far East spice trade, few Dutch seamen were ever unemployed. Some, however, sought fortunes of a different kind in the New World, where many were highly successful. One, who amassed a large booty, started to take it home in 1624, but, unfortunately, was wrecked in the Bahamas, where the remains of his ship and the treasure have been accidentally discovered recently by some skin divers.

To obtain a proper understanding of much that went on from the 16th century onwards it is necessary to appreciate the situation and the clear-cut issues which developed in Europe after the great impact of the Reformation, and how this affected seamen generally. When the English, together with the Dutch, the North Germans, and the Scandinavians, accepted the Reformation all immediately incurred the hostility of Spain. Because of the present-day movement to unite Christendom it is important to appreciate that the Reformation was not so much concerned with a reform of doctrines as with the unseemly lavish living and behaviour of many clerics in the religious houses. Spain, however, took upon herself, with Papal backing, a campaign against those it chose to call heretics. Protestant seamen, through no fault of their own, and particularly if they happened to be English, were seized while engaged on their lawful occasions around the Western European seaboard. Little wonder English public opinion was outraged, because we were not at war with Spain anyway. These unfortunate seamen were alleged to be trading in seas over which the Spaniards claimed a monopoly, and if caught were, at best, sentenced to work for years in galleys. Much more serious, however, were events if they ran foul of the ecclesiastical authorities commonly referred to as the Holy Office. If this happened they were subjected to the inhumanities of the Inquisition and even worse, the subsequent Auto da Fé (Act of Faith).

This Auto da Fé was actually staged by the civil authorities to carry out sentences imposed by the Holy Office. It cannot be overstressed that the majority of the English victims of all these horrors were simply illiterate seamen. Most shipmasters who got into trouble were ransomed or escaped from captivity by using the golden key. When news about the fate of their friends reached men on waterfronts around the British Isles it is understandable that there were many ready to go and teach Spain a lesson—as Drake put it, by singeing the King of Spain's beard—well before formal hostilities began with the Armada. Singeing the King's beard was probably an allusion to one of the torments practised at an Auto da Fé.

The Inquisition did not reach the New World until 1565, when it was established in Mexico because of the English depredations there. Later, other centres, or Palaces of the Inquisition as they were called, were set up in Cartagena (Colombia) and in Lima (Peru), where the Holy Office behaved just as despicably towards the indigenous inhabitants of the New World as it did to Europeans who incurred its displeasure. When, in later years, the pirates operating in the New World almost dominated the local scene, they treated the Spaniards, including many clerics, to a large and usually fatal dose of their own medicine. In the years before the Inquisition got busy in the New World, most European prisoners taken by the Spaniards were made slaves or sent to work in the local mines. This did not invariably happen, because, somewhat surprisingly, the relationship between the Spaniards and the various other European pirates operating in the New World occasionally seems to have been one of mutual respect; to the extent that if Spanish prisoners of importance were being held to ransom or exchange, any pirate prisoners were likely to be treated with some degree of humanity. Apart from such occasions Spaniards were regarded as implacable enemies to be sought out and destroyed as often as possible. About the middle of the 17th century, during the height of pirate activity and almost its domination of the Central American region, the Spaniards put it about that pirates sometimes ate their prisoners. Whatever excesses these men were guilty of there is no evidence that they ever fell quite as low as this.

The diabolical bloodless tortures (the Holy Office forbade the shedding of blood) used by the Inquisition have been fully described,[1] but not so the worse acts of the Spanish civil authorities at the Auto da Fé. Such events more than anything else made sailors of all nationalities enemies of the Spaniards, because so many of their fellows suffered.

The Auto da Fé has been called the last act of the inquisitional tragedy. At this affair, prisoners convicted by the Holy Office, often after extorted confessions, were handed over to the civil authorities for punishment which usually meant burning. Those who were sentenced to be strangled before being burnt could count themselves fortunate. The rest were chained and taken to an open space where there were as many stakes as there were prisoners. To ensure the presence of a large jeering crowd of all ages and sexes, a Sunday or Feast Day was chosen for the spectacle. The stakes used were about 3.75m. high with a small board near the top for the pinioned prisoners to be seated upon after being raised on a ladder. After repeated exhortations by Jesuit attendants to recant they were finally told that the Devil was standing at their elbow and waiting to receive their souls in hell. At this the crowd shouted 'Let the dogs' beard be made'. This involved the thrusting of burning furze on the end of poles against the faces of the victims until they were blackened, which caused the first applause from the crowd. Finally the fuel at the bottom of the stake was ignited. The prisoners were, however, so high up that the flames rarely reached beyond the seat, and they were roasted rather than burnt. As was recorded at the time, understandable cries for pity merely evoked more yells of satisfaction from the spectators. With this sort of fate in store for them need there be any wonder about the traditional last order of Sir Richard Grenville in *Revenge*: 'Sink her, Master Gunner, split her in twain, let us fall into the hands of God rather than the hands of Spain'.

Not to be outdone by Spain claiming all the New World and elsewhere for themselves, the French obtained local overseas footholds quite early, particularly in Canada, a territory they later lost in fair fight during the Seven Years War 200 years ago. Further south in the West Indies there was a French West India Company (very similar to the English Charter Companies such as the Massachusetts Company and the East India Company). The French were not permitted to be very successful colonists, as they were ruthlessly attacked by the Spaniards who resented any intrusion into what they regarded as their own preserve. In Europe the two countries were officially at peace! The original French colony in St. Kitts was practically exterminated, but the survivors fled to Hispaniola, later moving to the adjacent island of Tortuga which became the base for operations, mainly piratical, against the Spaniards.

This was the start of the buccaneers, and their story is told later on.

Apart from out-and-out 'bad 'uns', there have always been men about, just as there are today, ready to make a bit on the side by unscrupulous means. The modern safe-breaker's labourer is tempted at the week-end to perform some heavy task by the cash inducement from a gang of thieves, yet during the week he may well be engaged in what is regarded as respectable employment. Centuries ago, in a similar kind of way, seamen in European ports obviously put in a bit of piracy in northern waters on a part-time basis, as it were, when berths were difficult to find or trade was slack. Even a port like Bristol produced a quota. As late as 1716 a Bristol man named Fisher became a pirate captain, but nothing is recorded about his activities. Unemployment and trade depressions are not peculiar to the twentieth century. Such men were dishonest and ruthless, but many rogues are not necessarily unpleasant people when off duty.

In past days the ordinary man in an European seaport, or even inland, had little opportunity to better himself if he stayed put; if he went to sea the opportunites were much greater, and the further he went the greater they were. However, if a man went to sea he stayed there; he could not flit from job to job. Except during Stuart times and the French wars at the end of the 18th century, there were always more English sailors seeking berths than ships needing men. Once a man was in deep-sea navigation he was housed and fed and could earn reasonable wages—about two pounds monthly—supplemented by voyage bonuses, and sometimes prize money after a maritime fight. There was also considerable trading on the side, a practice permitted by all ship owners. It must have been these inducements which helped to make tolerable the notoriously bad conditions usual in most ships. Conditions were far worse than is realised, with leaking ships, bad food, and putrid diseases of all kinds in which scurvy predominated. If you were in a pirate ship much of this unpleasantness was avoided, except for a tendency to overcrowding; voyages were generally short and the victuals usually plentiful.

Pirates were always much better off financially than honest merchant seamen, even when trade was brisk. To live well always requires the money to do so, but both these groups of seamen were infinitely better off in every respect than their English contemporaries in Kings' ships. Until the 18th century there were few naval ships in regular commission; in wartime most navies were strengthened by using armed merchantmen, and conditions of life in these ships steadily deteriorated once they became government responsibility. However, life in privateers on lawful occasions seems to have been reasonably attractive, and probably was even better when these ships turned to piracy, as they so often did.

In far-off places men often turned pirate from necessity. When a merchantman was captured her crew was usually given the choice of joining the gang or being put over the side without ceremony. You can read about prisoners having to walk the plank, but I know of only one authentic account of such a practice. It concerns the Dane named Derdrake, who was originally a ship's carpenter, but later turned to piracy around the Baltic in about 1700. He was utterly ruthless and drowned all his prisoners, mostly by the plank method to prolong the agony. On one occasion he did even worse. A Russian lady taken prisoner proved to be the sister of the governor of St. Petersburg (Leningrad) who, for some reason, had incurred Derdrake's displeasure, something for which his sister could hardly be held responsible. Yet after various indignities he stabbed her to death in the back. The idea about plank-walking may have been popularised from its mention in Robert Louis Stevenson's *Treasure Island*. Possibly this famous writer obtained additional evidence upon which to base his story. Even that great authority on maritime history, C. B. Norman, writing 100 years ago, makes only one reference—and that disbelieving—to the practice.

When an ordinary merchant seaman was confronted with the choice between being put over the side or joining a gang it is obvious that many must have chosen the latter, perhaps with the thought that the future might present a chance to escape. It would soon be discovered that, once in a gang, the conduct of life was an all-or-nothing affair. There was no holding back—if you did you were shot. So unless you were dedicated, simply to join a gang was in itself not without risks. Still, one party of men forced into service managed to overpower their captors and escape to Boston, Massachusetts. The leader was John Fillmore, whose great-great-grandson, Millard Fillmore, became President of the United States in 1850. John Fillmore was an English Banks fisherman in a vessel attacked off Newfoundland when the choice was 'Join us or else . . .'.

Those prisoners were particularly welcomed, and called sea artists—men of ships' officer rank, or tradesmen such as carpenters, who might be persuaded to provide the technical help and skills pirates usually lacked. Always wanted was anyone who could navigate; such a man was termed a pilot. Pilots were normally responsible for the navigation of any ship, for which purpose they possessed their own instruments and nautical almanacs, such as they were. The urgent search for skilled help is understandable because the average pirate started life as an ordinary seaman, and, while highly competent as such, was usually quite unable to navigate.

Surgeons, too, were always in demand and well paid if they would join a gang, when, in addition to getting a share of any loot, they would be paid as much as 250 dollars a voyage. Generally speaking, any such surgeon was not required to sign articles of agreement if he was only required to undertake professional work. One surgeon actually signed articles, under different circumstances. He was Peter Scudamore of Bristol, originally surgeon in *Mercy,* a merchantman captured by Bartholomew Roberts of *Royal Fortune* in 1721. He expressed a wish to sign articles under Roberts in order to prove himself; thereafter he became for a while just an ordinary pirate. The new life obviously did not come up to his expectations, because while a member of a prize crew he tried to incite a mutiny; an offence which was detected. He had to face a rough and ready trial by his associates and, inevitably, was sentenced to be hanged. When d'Oberon was wounded during his unsuccessful attack on Puerto Rico in 1673 a French pirate surgeon was later called in to treat him.

Just why medical men, except when taken prisoner, were prepared to join pirate gangs is hard to explain. At the time we are considering there were few fully trained and qualified doctors as we understand them today, yet there were a number of men who had gained a limited experience of practical medicine, or, more correctly, surgery, while acting as surgeon's mates in naval vessels and the larger merchantmen. Many of them, not required to observe any special ethical or professional rules, must have been attracted by the excitement of a rover's life. On some lucrative shore expeditions, particularly on the West Coast of South America, surgeons often shed their professional mantle and joined ordinary gangs on the currently accepted terms and rules.

Even the Church provided a quota (albeit limited) of recruits to piracy. On one occasion a man named Mussin teamed up with a renegade Italian priest in a French frigate off Martinique, where they staged a successful mutiny. All the officers were killed and the ship was simply sailed off to be one more in the Caribbean pirate fleet.

Many prisoners were taken during shore raids on the Spanish Main. They were always treated harshly if reluctant to act as guides or to provide needed local information concerning the whereabouts of treasure or military dispositions. A favourite torture was to stretch them: this consisted of suspending the victim by his arms from the branch of a tree, and tying stones to his feet until he talked. Stretching was a simple form of the rack used frequently by the Holy Office on its victims, and many ecclesiastics were deliberately stretched so that they could experience personally what it felt like. Stretching gave a prisoner time to make up his mind whether to talk, but usually after he talked he was run through with a cutlass for holding up the proceedings. Another fatal torture was to impale the prisoner on a stake passed through the anus and up the body.

As we have seen already, on occasions there were reasons other than greed for assuming the life of a pirate. It was a a love affair in the case of Alvilda, as mentioned later in this chapter. Matrimonial discord caused at least one Londoner to leave his home, but judging by his subsequent behaviour our sympathies should be for his wife. Thomas Howard started life as a Thames lighterman, and then became a deep-water sailor after domestic trouble of his own making. In time he met the famous Captain Bowen, sometimes known as the Gentleman Adventurer of Bermuda. Bowen, after a long and successful career as a captain for American shipowners, fell into the hands of pirates in the Indian Ocean, and decided to become one himself. He chose Howard to be his quartermaster, to act as a liaison officer between the crew and the captain. Since a captain held his position by election, except when some forceful character recruited a gang with himself as captain, he was not too secure and often depended for his safety upon faithful henchmen. After various adventures, Howard, who was generally acknowledged to be able but unscrupulous, progressed sufficiently by 1701 to become Captain Howard of *Prosperous,* a 36-gun ex-East Indiaman, which he had captured and adapted for his own purposes. In this well-armed ship he successfully operated for a long time off the coasts of India where he married a wealthy Indian woman and settled down. Finally, because he treated his Indian wife so abominably, he was murdered by one of her relations: no one appears to have been surprised by the manner of his end.

Then there were those who, as it would be expressed nowadays, were wanted by the police for some offence and whom deemed it wiser to get out of the country and practise their dishonesty elsewhere. Two pickpockets did this about 1700, and there is more about one of them on page 125. In the Caribbean and along the Pacific Coast, which could hardly be bettered as regions for piracy, there was never any shortage of recruits of all nationalities to what was called the Brotherhood of the Main.

One group of men who could get mixed up with pirates were the gentlemen adventurers. These we first hear about in the time of Drake, who had several in *Golden Hind.* Similar men with private means from other European countries, like the Frenchman De Mont, were equally adventurous. But the great difference between those of Continental origin and their English counterparts was that the former thought it beneath their dignity to help in working the ship, a job they regarded as only suitable for common sailors. Drake would have none of this, and the gentlemen in his ship had to perform any task assigned to them on board: 'The gentlemen to haul and draw with the mariner, and the mariner with the gentlemen'. Apart from gentlemen adventurers who participated in properly organised voyages, there were some who went overseas on their own, simply for an adventurous life. One, named Basil Ringrose, had this in full measure, spending about five years in and around the Darien Peninsula and the northern parts of South America. He was part author of the well-known book by Esquemeling which describes much of the goings-on there for several years. He was killed during an affray ashore in Mexico in 1686.

One question of great interest is to what extent there were women in pirate ships. Since it is clearly recorded that certain captains would not permit women in their ships, it also seems that some captains did not object to them; but whether this was when a ship was at sea or while in port is obscure.

The rise of northern European piracy is generally ascribed to the Norsemen, but at an earlier period the Goths, living in which is now north Germany, practised it on a small scale. One of the most celebrated Goth pirates was a woman. Her name was Alvilda, daughter of a king of the Goths in southern Sweden, named Sypardus. She went to sea to escape the tribulation of an enforced marriage with Alf, son of Sigarus, king of Denmark. Her first crew consisted of young women, who must have been a tough bunch, since all ships were then propelled as much by oars as by sail. It may seem strange, even in the present day of feminine emancipation, that a crew of women could not only navigate but also fight a ship successfully on the high seas. However, during the French wars in the time of Henry VIII one of the chief sources of trained seamen for royal ships was the fisherman in the

West County. In their absence the fishing smacks were
worked by their women who 'handled oar, sail and net'.
Still, they had no fighting to do. After successful initial
voyages Alvilda met another pirate crew which had recently
lost their captain and, as they were obviously impressed by her
efficiency, she was made chief of a combined gang. This
gang became renowned for its prowess, and, in due course,
Prince Alf of Denmark, unaware of the identity of its
captain, determined to attack it at sea. Alf's ship was beaten
off for some time, but eventually he prevailed and boarded
Alvilda's vessel, killing most of the crew. He seized the
captain and removed the casque then worn, to discover the
identity of the wearer. Under these unusual circumstances he
again proposed, a proposal which this time was accepted.[2]

Apart from women in more recent times, like Anne
Bonney, who became a famous commander, and her later
companion, Mary Read, there must have been many women
eager to go to sea either to be with their man, or simply
for the adventure. Under one pretext or another many
women went to sea in men-of-war during the 18th century,
and were just as brave in battle as the men. The women in
these men-of-war came from various British ports, but
who the women were in Caribbean pirate ships and where
they came from we shall never know; perhaps a few were
some of the Irish women that Cromwell suggested should
be sent to Jamaica to help populate the new English colony.

Still, it must be remembered that early in the 16th century
Europeans started colonising the New World, a region to
become the homeland for many families in which there must
have been adventurous women.

After the story about Alvilda I know of no mention of
women until the time of the great activity in and around
the Caribbean in the 17th century, and later in the Indian
Ocean. It is quite obvious that women were often in ships,
but whether they were there just for social purposes or
something else is unknown. The fact that so much is known
about Anne Bonney and Mary Read suggests, perhaps, that
their particular activities were exceptional; just how they
became pirates bears repeating. Anne Bonney was the

daughter of an Irish lawyer who emigrated to Carolina and prospered. Anne became secretly married to a sailor in Charlestown after her father had forbidden the match. When he heard about it Anne was cut off with a shilling instead of the dowry she and her husband expected, so they took themselves off to New Providence in the Bahamas. There her marriage broke up in 1719, and she met John Rackham (Calico Jack), a well-known rover, whom she married and went to sea with to share his life. Soon she became as equally competent with a cutlass as with a marline-spike, and before long was leading boarding parties when they attacked ships. Some time later she met Mary Read, an equally lively character, in a ship captured by Rackham.

Mary Read was born in London, and, having to make her own way in the world, hid her sex and shipped in a man-of-war. After a while she deserted and joined the army in Europe where she married a trooper; the couple obtained their discharge and then kept an inn. Unfortunately, her husband died, so Mary went to sea again, and she finally joined forces with Anne Bonney and Captain Rackham. During this time she even fought a successful duel. In 1720 Rackham's ship was attacked by a British frigate off Jamaica and boarded, when a fierce fight took place in which Anne and Mary played a leading part; eventually they were overpowered and taken prisoner. Both women were tried in Jamaica and sentenced to death, but Mary Read escaped the gallows by dying in prison from natural causes; whether Anne Bonney actually was executed is unknown.

The late Doctor Hope Gosse told a remarkable story about a Dutch pirate, Hiram Breakes, who worked the coast of Spain and the Western Mediterranean in the mid 18th century. On one occasion he sighted a nunnery near the shore in Minorca, and suggested to his crew that they should all fit themselves out with wives. Headed by their captain the crew went up to the door where they were greeted by the Lady Abbess; they entered, each selected a nun and returned to the ship. Soon after this incident Breakes quit the sea and went back to Holland, where he had a legal wife whom he found had been hanged in his absence for poisoning their son. Comment is needless.

Notes

1. *Torquamada and the Spanish Inquisition.* Sabatini. 1913.
2. *Encyclopaedia Britannica.* 1792.

CHAPTER VII

THE PIRATE PERSONALITY

THE ABSENCE OF RECORDS makes it impossible to do otherwise than speculate about the personal backgrounds of men who became pirates long ago. But we know sufficient about the social history and the social structure in more recent times of our own and other European countries to make it possible to visualise the personality of men we are considering, its relationship with the life they led, and their reasons for adopting it. There were occasions for an upsurge in piracy involving men who in the ordinary course of events might otherwise have led perfectly honest lives, but who became the victims of circumstances as described in the previous chapter.

The outlook of ordinary folk in the past resembled in many respects that of folk today, indeed, greed and selfishness are just as widespread now, if not worse, because many look to others to provide them with a living. It is very apparent that life for the majority in many countries, even when people are provided with its basic necessities, can be monotonous, and various means are taken, unconsciously perhaps, to break the monotony. To do so rewardingly is, of course, an intellectual exercise, and often various forms of violence are substituted by those ill-equipped mentally to undertake this exercise. Such ways of breaking monotony can manifest themselves as a mass affair with riots or demonstrations, for which the London mob was so renowned for centuries (and, perhaps still is), or in the past individuals becoming pirates. While we may deplore the pirate way of life it is salutory to remember it was recently announced in Parliament that, annually, nearly two thousand youths between the ages of 14 and 21 are convicted of robbery with violence.[1]

Most pirates had no education, no certainty of employment, men then had to beg their bread if they had not got a job. In contrast, modern gangsters have had public money spent on their education and never live within a few days of possible starvation.

In the times when piracy was widespread in European countries, including the British Isles, human life was cheap; killings were frequent, and many crimes not now regarded very seriously, because of better social conditions, were punishable by death. Even contemporary judicial executions reflected this attitude towards human life. Frequently such events were not the straightforward affair of a beheading or a hanging: several heads might be stuck up in public places as a warning to others, while hanging could be harsher by subsequent drawing and quartering of the prisoners, often done while the victims were still alive. What must have been a macabre situation at any time was made even worse after one of the mass executions which took place occasionally in this country; then executioners are known to have complained because they were not issued with sufficient firewood to burn all the guts of those sentenced to be drawn and quartered. There is no wonder that boys reared in such an atmosphere must have been influenced for life; and, if they became pirates, they would suffer no pangs of conscience about what they saw going on. If a companion was killed they were sorry, but quite aware that their turn might come soon; so what matter? Such an attitude to death has been seen again recently despite the benefits of an improved social environment. I would refer to the attitude to life expressed by some of the mods and rockers who were tearing along the roads a few years ago. A number of these youths were seriously injured, some fatally, in attempts to achieve 'a ton up' (i.e., 100 m.p.h.) with powerful motor cycles on ordinary roads. One badly injured youth I saw, whose friend had been killed, remarked what matter if he had been killed, he must take his chance like everyone else.

Sailors went to sea as boys, and usually were able seamen by the time they were seventeen. Their life as fit men was short: anyone who reached 30 was regarded as an old man. As I understand it, most ordinary pirates were in their late teens or early 20s; though captains, with a few notable exceptions, were somewhat older—in their 30s or early 40s. The captain of a Spanish vessel captured in the Pacific by Drake, during his circumnavigation of the world, spent a week as prisoner on board *Golden Hind* before he was released. He submitted a report on the experience to his government, in which, among other matters, he commented on the general youthfulness of Drake's crew and the number of boys, and also how well the ship was provided with sea-stores.

Since we know that men are as time is, and that the heart of man does not change very much, it can be assumed from ancient writings about the widespread cruelties then existing and accepted that the backgrounds and personalities of pirates in the remote past must have resembled those of their successors in more recent times. The pity is that we know next to nothing about those actually engaged in ancient piracy.

The treatment of prisoners in some ways reflects the general, and sometimes unpredictable, attitude to life of the pirate gangs, and the fate of many who would not join them has already been described. For no reason that I can discover, beyond the fact that extra labour was needed for a job, some prisoners were occasionally considered to be harmless and just put to work on ship repairs or such tasks at a base.

Some prisoners might even be regarded as unsuitable recruits because their ship carried no cargo worth stealing and the vessel itself was unattractive. But this did not mean that, after being taken prisoner, her crew necessarily went scot free. These unfortunates might have their ears cut off, apparently for the fun of it, or be used to provide material for a brutal game called sweating. The procedure was this: below the main deck, where the mizzen mast passed through the orlop deck, a close circle of lighted candles was arranged allowing sufficient space for a man to pass round between the candles and the mast. When the first prisoner was in position, he was surrounded by his captors who prodded him with forks or anything conveniently sharp and was forced to go round and round the confined space to a musical accompaniment. After about ten minutes of this treatment he collapsed from sheer heat and exhaustion and was forcibly removed. Then another victim was put through the same process until there had been sufficient entertainment. As a final act of clemency the men were allowed to return to their own ships as best they could. Another and rather pointless pastime was to make a prisoner eat candles. Women prisoners must have had a trying time: one ship taken off Martinique had a single woman passenger, and 21 men forced their attentions on her; eventually her back was broken and she was thrown overboard.

I have never seen any authentic account of keel-hauling in modern times by pirates; possibly it was too elaborate a procedure for them to bother with. They had handier ways of inflicting torture punishment. Keel-hauling seems to have been a very old form of punishment at sea as it is portrayed on an ancient Greek vase in Athens. Whether it was out of compassion to get the drowning of prisoners over quickly, or whether it was just to ensure they were drowned before any possibility of escape, one captain used to tie double round shot to their necks. This man, Thwaites, was originally an officer in the British Navy who deserted his ship off Algiers about 1760 and entered the service of the Bey to organise Mediterranean piracy for him. This he did for 20 years, and made a fortune. Part of this he somehow managed to remit to his wife in England; the rest he used to buy an estate near New York to which he ultimately retired.

Dealing with recalcitrant prisoners was, on the whole, a short and sharp affair, but sometimes it could be tinged with prolonged cold-blooded sadism. For instance, a prisoner might be hauled with a plain tackle into the rigging which was then released so that he crashed down to immediate death on the deck, or to death shortly afterwards from multiple injuries. If a prisoner were slow in parting with some needed information his dispatch would be proceeded by various mutilations to try to make him talk. On occasion prisoners might be stripped and, after rings had been painted on them, used for target practice with small arms. Another procedure sometimes used on important prisoners, held to ransom or exchange, and about whom negotiations nearby were considered to be unduly prolonged, was to bind them bent over the muzzles of loaded guns in full view of all concerned. Then if no progress were being made one or more of the guns would be fired. That dead men tell no tales was a necessary doctrine on many occasions; if you didn't subscribe to it you were liable to be reported to be operating in a region and possibly caught and executed, while likely prizes in the neighbourhood might be warned of danger.

A distinguished psychiatrist once explained to me the mental processes underlying sadism towards prisoners, and, in particular, the reason why the sexual organs were parts usually mutilated first during the horrible progress round the bodies of victims. For people with limited understanding and education all aspects of sex are dominant, particularly the sexual act, in conversation and in stories; this priority contrasts sharply with the thinking of more cultured people, with their divers interests. The contrast, probably more evident centuries ago, still exists. Sodomy was accepted practice at sea in ordinary merchantmen, so there is no reason to suppose that the state of affairs was any different in a pirate ship, where coarse living and brutality were accepted. Ashore, sodomy was punishable by death.

It is easy to understand what happened, when, particularly in the Caribbean, young men could suddenly become extremely wealthy. Lack of education or social stability denied them any possible way of enjoying their wealth other than with carnal pleasures. However, for free time to be spent in such fashion was nothing new; in ancient times the Mediterranean pirates would feast ashore after their austere life at sea, while the Norsemen lived lavishly on their spoils and spent the winter evenings in drinking bouts, at which mead was the favourite beverage: other things followed. Such a pattern of life was reproduced in the various Viking settlements around the European coasts where, it appears, their insatiable demand for women could be easily satisfied. No woman was ever allowed on board a Viking ship.

The gaming-houses and brothels in Tortuga and Jamaica in the 17th century make places like Las Vegas today resemble country garden-parties. Think of it: £10,000 in cash available on the spur of the moment to tempt a popular whore to stand stripped on a table. If cash ran short, which it often did within a few days, then a man might offer instead an emerald or other precious stone, assessing its value at a few pounds, whereas its true value might be a thousand pounds or more. A daylight sport at Port Royal in Jamaica was shark catching. Men would dive in the water near sharks and kill them by sticking bodkins into their bellies. Some were mutilated or killed during this hazardous pastime, but such risks were accepted as part of the sport. As will be explained later on, all this sort of thing was not so manifest in the eastern seas. Men were, to some extent, able to integrate with the long-established local ways of life, which was impossible in the New World, where all the old civilisations had been destroyed by the Spaniards.

The average pirate anywhere must have been immensely strong. He had to be in order for such feats to have been achieved by boarding parties: after climbing up a ship's side they were then confronted with fierce opposition. Yet we know certainly that a few hundred years ago sailors, like other men at that time, were not particularly big, something which emerges from the detailed measurements in a list I possess of those wanted after the *Bounty* mutiny in 1789.

How strong some were, or perhaps, more correctly, they became as a result of their vigorous life, can be understood from the fact that ashore some seamen could carry three or four hundredweight apparently without much difficulty; as, for instance, when a stolen cargo of logwood had to be manhandled for loading. Then again, after successful shore raids of various kinds had been undertaken, each man might have to carry a quantity of gold or specie in addition to his ordinary equipment; gold is heavy stuff. After some of the shore raids in the New World mules had to be found somehow to transport the heavy loot; when there were no mules, prisoners would be used as porters.

Much of this laborious work was in the tropics, often in places beset with diseases which even now have not lost their terrors. The death rate among Europeans overseas from malaria, yellow fever and suchlike was appalling, yet the buccaneers of the New World and pirates did not suffer too badly despite the hardships they often endured. Recurrent attacks of malaria hardly promote physical fitness in anybody, yet when a buccaneer was asked how he was he would politely reply, 'Quite well, thank you, but for the fever'. One thing that made the European colonist more prone to local disease was living ashore, and therefore more or less continuously in contact with the mosquitoes which transmit tropical fevers. Pirates, on the other hand, spent much of their time afloat away from these insect pests. As time passed and yellow fever spread in the New World, to which it was imported from Central Africa by slaves, the disease became disastrous to fresh European arrivals. The one redeeming feature of the disease was that the ability to survive an initial attack provided protection against any subsequent one, as body immunity was thereby established. As early as 1688 Sir Hans Sloane refers to local fevers, possibly not always of the same variety, being collectively called the seasoning, a term which became widely adopted in the New World.

Just how the Caribbean pirates acquired sufficient immunity against many serious diseases as to permit the recruitment of adequate numbers for successful shore raids, often against Spanish soldiers and even forts, was explained by the late General Gorgas. He was the United States officer in charge of the health services during the construction of the Panama Canal early in the present century. His successful public health rules enabled the Americans to build a canal, which earlier had proved an impossible feat to the French, owing to the local diseases, particularly yellow fever. During the years he spent in Panama he made a special study of the health of the buccaneers. He described in a lecture (unfortunately never fully published) how, quite early, the buccaneers discovered for themselves the principle of salting. We hear nowadays about troops operating in tropical climates needing to be seasoned or salted before becoming fit for active service. This seasoning is the acquisition of natural immunity or protection from local infections likely to be encountered for the first time, and which cannot all be completely prevented by inoculation. Any new arrivals in the region who wished to join up with a gang were required to undergo a period of acclimatisation. This was achieved at small shore bases with a good water supply where parties of men would be landed, with adequate basic stores of food and ammunition, and left to fend for themselves for several months. During that time they would almost certainly contract malaria and yellow fever, and probably a flux as well. If they succumbed to one or other of the diseases it was unfortunate; if they survived, then that was the object of the exercise. With rare exceptions immunity to malaria cannot be acquired, but these men were encouraged to regard attacks much in the way we regard ordinary common colds. When a pirate captain needed extra hands in his ship for a predatory cruise he sailed round and picked up the men he wanted. Sometimes, when news reached one of these places that a ship was 'fitting out' at one of the usual bases, a number of the salted seamen would find their own way in a canoe or by any means available to join the new venture. To have a good supply of salted men available was seen to best advantage when any big shore raid was contemplated to attack one of the important Spanish towns or cities; then the leader would cruise round with his consorts to make up crews to full strength. When Morgan staged his attack on Cartagena in 1670 his men cannot have been properly seasoned, because many suffered from jaundice (yellow fever) of the serious kind called black jaundice. Some victims of this usually fatal form of the disease were alleged to have been cured by an infusion of goose dung, but this seems unlikely!

Morgan's men were also desperately short of food and were even forced to eat their leather satchels. How this was done was described afterwards by a man who was there: 'Some persons who never were out of their mother's kitchens may ask how pirates could eat, swallow and digest those pieces of leather, so hard and dry: unto whom I only answer: That could they ever experience what hunger, or rather famine, is they would certainly find the manner by their own necessity, as the pirates did. For these first took the leather, and sliced it in pieces. Then did they beat it between two stones, and rub it often dipping it in water to render it by these means supple and tender. Lastly they scraped off the hair, and roasted it or broiled it upon the fire. And, being thus cooked, they cut it into small morsels, and eat it, helping it down with frequent gulps of water'.

Piecing together the information on the pirates who were of European nationality working the Guinea Coast and the Indian Ocean sets them apart, in many ways, from their brothers in crime elsewhere. The nature of the waters over which they sailed required higher standards of seamanship than needed in seas like the Caribbean: in the Indian Ocean cruises lasted many months or even a year. In that ocean it is evident that guns were used occasionally, and gun crews in any ship had to submit to regular practices and some degree of discipline if they were to be at all effective. We know well enough that discipline of any kind was not a strong point, so at least some of the men must have differed from the ordinary run-of-the-mill thug. This said, it is evident that they were no less ruthless and bloodthirsty than their counterparts anywhere else.

Piracy along the Guinea Coast, although quite active, never reached the proportions attained elsewhere. Still, owners of ships in the slave trade must have regarded the situation serious enough at the time, because their ships, outward-bound with general cargoes, suffered badly. From the purely operational aspect the Guinea Coast had little to recommend it. Even the crews of honest merchantmen discharging cargo or loading slaves were fully aware of the risks of malaria or yellow fever always menacing them, in an area soon to be designated the White Man's Grave. For pirates the chance of making a packet must have compensated for the continuous health risks incurred. Although at sea the risk of catching these mosquito-borne diseases was minimal, when ships anchored in any river mouth near swampy land pirates succumbed as readily as anybody else. How they could suffer on occasions is well exemplified in Chapter XI.

The absence of any towns along the coast other than simple trading settlements did not provide the pleasures and excitements expected as part of a chosen way of life, particularly for any who knew what Port Royal and Tortuga had to offer. It is significant that many who transferred to the Guinea Coast after being expelled from Central America in 1689 did not remain there very long before moving round to the Indian Ocean to join the Madagascar fraternity. The small islands in the Cape Verde group, often used as bases by Guinea pirates, while having good natural features, cannot have been very exciting places for young men. Some men actually returned to selected places in the New World and worked the New England coast, or made direct forays across the Atlantic to Guinea.

The ravages by Europeans in the Indian Ocean and the Arabian Sea during the 17th and 18th centuries had special features because of the prolonged deep-sea voyages involved, but these were from good bases in Madagascar, which also provided something approaching a social life ashore. How different the men were from those in other parts of the world is hard to judge; still the very nature of their occupations makes it unlikely that they were clean-living chaps. However, the opportunities for real excesses were limited. Bourbon (Réunion) had its attractions, but no other recreational place was noteworthy. Further east, Tong King, in Indo-China, was patronised mainly by merchant seamen. The sort of place it was is conveyed by the 1660 description by Dampier: 'Yet the common bawdy-house, though extremely rife here, are by all of them (the patrons) accounted "hateful and scandalous" '.

Madagascar as an operational base was in some respects unique. Here was a very large island; the Malagasy population, possessing strong Arab infusions, had maintained contact with the outside world since Roman times (the Menathinas of Ptolemy, A.D. 139), and earlier. The climate and soil were good, and the natural resources ample; so when pirates started visiting and using the place they were not on some remote island with barbarous inhabitants. As the Abbé Rochon wrote: 'The Madagascar people always live in society; that is to say in towns and villages . . . the houses of private people consist of a convenient cottage . . . the houses of the great are very spacious'. He also remarks how the Malagasy were remarkably free from the excesses in their manner of life, a contrast from the manner in which many civilised nations conducted themselves at the time. Despite inevitable ups and downs it seems very likely that life in Madagascar provided that 'something' which pirates must often unknowingly have sought but rarely, if ever, found. Between voyages life ashore was almost domestic in character, and many who quit the sea settled down successfully. To do so in Europe was out of the question because of the risk of arrest, while in the New World, largely occupied by the Spaniards, and to a limited extent by other European Powers, there were no longstanding communities with whom permanent association could be established.

Although the French always tried, unsuccessfully, to dominate the local scene in Madagascar, the pirates who were English must have behaved very well ashore and exerted considerable influence. When Admiral Watson visited the island in 1754 he found that English names and customs were common among responsible people with whom he had dealings, and that a patois English was spoken in several coastal settlements.[2]

Most European piracy in the Far East was conducted from Madagascar, possibly because of the inevitable health risk at shore bases in the Eastern Archipelago and Malaya. Here serious fluxes were prevalent, and little immunity could be established against them in the way possible with some other tropical diseases. Residents in the Dutch settlement scattered around suffered badly, and visiting ships in those parts avoided direct shore contact as far as possible. The indigenous population did not suffer by any means as much as the Europeans, probably because they had inherent immunity to disease devasting to Europeans, honest or dishonest.

Despite their skill as seamen, the pirates' complete lack of discipline must have endangered many a ship. This ill-discipline was apparent even on passages, when some ordinary navigational hazard could not be overcome in a seamanlike fashion. Dampier refers to this in his voyage around Cape Horn in 1684, when the ocean passage had to be taken to reach the Pacific simply because the men could not be relied upon to act with sufficient alertness to sail the ship successfully through the Straits of Magellan. Yet when it came to catching a likely prize and manoeuvring into the correct position for boarding, discipline must have been good to achieve such consistently good results.[3]

Notes

1. *Hansard,* 25 October 1972.
2. *Voyage to India,* Ives. 1760.
3. *loc. cit.*

CHAPTER IX

HOW THEY OPERATED

BEFORE FIREARMS came to be used in sea-fights there was no means of hurling missiles at an opponent except by bows and arrows, and a Roman stone-throwing device called the *tormenta bellica*. Ships laid alongside each other and hand-to-hand fighting ensued. The basic concept of ordinary naval engagements had always been that one ship fought another ship, and the crews were concerned that their ship put up a good fight; any soldiers fighting afloat instead of ashore could almost be regarded as part of the ship's armament.

Such a concept of naval actions did not apply when pirates were concerned; they made a direct attack on the crew of a potential prize by boarding as quickly as possible. In Mediterranean operations in remote times, it appears that ships were regarded as a means of transport, and in no way as naval vessels. To have been able to board and capture a prize, often when greatly outnumbered, must have demanded ruthlessness unsurpassed by any other fighting men, and there is no reason to suppose that in antiquity it was all any less bloodthirsty than in later times. Much is known about the ruthlessness of the Vikings, the like of which had never been seen before. These men actually set the original pattern for piracy in Northern Europe, and it may well be that their successors followed their example in the ruthlessness for which they were so notorious, right up until final suppression.

Anything in the way of a pitched battle between a pirate ship and a likely prize was avoided, because the former would come off badly in an ordinary battle with any ship having expertly-served guns. The only time that anything approaching an engagement of this kind occurred was in the Indian Ocean in the days of the Madagascar pirates, when men like Edward England and the Frenchman, Surcouf, were sailing with reasonably well-disciplined crews and gunners (see Chapter XIV). Nevertheless, these captains always boarded their prizes as soon as possible, after getting their bows over an opponent in a special manner, peculiar to pirate practice, to be described.

Though piracy was conducted from ordinary ocean-going ships adapted for the purpose, it will have been understood already how much could be achieved from small boats or small vessels used simply to convey boarding parties. This method of attack was started in early Mediterranean days when a gang would push out from some sheltered creek to attack a becalmed merchantman, or one anchored for the night somewhere inshore, a method also favoured by Malays and others in recent times for attacking traders in the Eastern Archipelago.

When guns came to be the chief armament, ship design had to be adjusted to meet the requirements for gunnery; special provision was made for mounting guns securely and sufficiently low so as not to affect the stability of ships. One result was to make the increasing cost of arming and manning ocean-going vessels such that it could only be met from Government funds, or by wealthy men collaborating to fit out large merchantmen or privateers. While pirates always employed their favoured boarding technique, the time came when they required ships capable of deep sea navigations if anything more than coasting was contemplated. Thus it came about in Europe that the fitting-out of suitable vessels was done quite openly in various ports; indeed, in some ports around the British Isles it looks as if piracy was regarded as almost a subsidiary local industry. It is otherwise difficult to imagine how ships could be fitted out and commissioned, always a costly business, and sufficiently good crews found to man them. This is an instance of what happened in Woodbridge, Suffolk, during the reign of Elizabeth I, where lived a man named Thomas Leckford. He was a prosperous shipowner, with interests on the East

Coast, and he also participated in the public life of London where he was received at Court. Yet it is known that at least one of his ships was engaged in piracy. And we have already seen how some Englishmen obtained ships with French assistance.

After various hotspots were finally suppressed early in the 17th century, piracy declined in European waters except in the western Mediterranean, where corsairs continued to operate freely from the North African coast. Overseas, however, it broke out with renewed vigour, chiefly in the New World where such lucrative prizes could be found. There the natural aptitude of Frenchmen at hand-to-hand fighting made them particularly formidable.

The English sea rovers in Elizabethan times used naval guns in their ships, and the early attention given to the potentialities of naval gunnery resulted in an increasing number of men about the seaports able to serve guns. This skill not only helped to check Spanish aggression against England, but was useful when ships turned to piracy. But after the danger to England was over, the use of naval guns in pirate ships declined. There were, however, some captains during the next hundred years or so who trained men to serve the smaller kinds of guns: none with a bore exceeding 10cm. (i.e., 18 pounders) were used, since they needed five or six men to serve them properly. Apart from the constant drill necessary to serve even small guns efficiently, the number of men required could create a drain on the manpower in any ship. As a working rule a man was needed for every 254 kilos of armament.

The safety of many merchantmen in distant seas depended upon good armament which was more than a match for the occasional pirate ship with any gunners. There are just a few instances of gun duels almost amounting to naval battles taking place. The best known involved *Prosperous,* an ex-East Indiaman, commanded by Captain Howard, former Thames lighterman; and the battle between Edward England, with *Fancy* and *Victory,* and the East Indiaman, *Cassandra,* Captain Mackray (see page 158).

It is remarkable that, apart from making them shorter, there were no material alterations in the design of guns

and the methods of use from the time they were introduced into the Western World from China in the 15th
century, until they were finally outdated in the 19th
century. They were all heavy and cumbersome; and, indeed,
field pieces could not exceed 18-pounders, and usually were
much smaller. At sea, then, as now, it was possible to use
big guns, some as large as the 48-pounders in ships of the
line; but for defending merchantmen and, by implication,
in pirate ships, only the small calibres were practicable.
Originally even the small calibre guns were 2.5 or 2.8 metres
long, and not until some were accidentally cast too short was
it discovered that these were equally efficient and much
more manageable. Rather after the manner of giving names
to various church bells, so different guns were named to
distinguish the sizes; eventually all guns came to be designated by the weight of shot fired. Only one, the culverin,
retained its name and became a term often used to signify
a slender handy gun fitted on the deck of merchantmen to
help repel boarding parties with grape shot.

Since there is little mention of these names in popular
books this old list (giving contemporary weights) is of
interest in connection with the subject of merchant ship
armament.

			pdr.	cwt.
Whole Culverin	..	..	18	50
Demi Culverin	..	..	9	30
Falcon	..	..	6	25
Sacker Largest	..	..	8	18
·Ordinary	..	..	6	15
Lowest sort	..	..	5	13
Dragon	..	..	6	12
Serpentine ..	..	..	4	8
Aspic	..	..	2	7
Falconet.. ..	..	..	3, 2, 1	15, 10, 5

Guns of larger calibre only used in men-of-war were also named.

For several centuries guns were cast in gun-metal, an
alloy of copper, brass and tin, and the actual proportions
of these ingredients used by various gun-founders was a
closely-guarded secret. In course of time, as the methods

for casting iron were improved, this could replace gun-metal with a substantial saving in weight.

The expeditious serving of guns at sea was not only heavy work, but was quite an elaborate affair with all the mopping out, charging, ramming and laying, so constant practice was needed to achieve a good rate of fire. Plate 3, taken from an old print, shows the tools needed to service a gun properly. At sea it was always difficult to achieve real accuracy, and, though a cannon ball could carry a mile or more, ship fights took place at short range. One method of reducing the deflection of cannon balls in flight, and therefore increasing accuracy, was devised by a Frenchman late in the 17th century, and termed the '*batterie à ricochet*'. This could be used effectively at water level at sea as well as on land; indeed, Nelson used it on occasions. Probably the most far-reaching application of the principle in history was made by Dr. Barnes Wallis (the late Sir Barnes Wallis), when he devised the special bombs in 1943 for the Royal Air Force to breach the big Ruhr dams successfully and do so much to cripple German war production. *Plus ça change plus c'est la même chose.*

Pirates used small arms devastatingly in their own special forms of attack, brought to perfection firstly in the Caribbean and later in the Indian Ocean. Their skill with small arms was even admired by the professional soldiers. Some time after Morgan with his rough bunch of seamen had successfully attacked and looted the important and well-defended port of Porto Bello, on the Atlantic seaboard of the Panama Isthmus, the Spanish governor of the equally important city of Panama on the Pacific side sent Morgan a message. He asked if he could be given some small pattern of the arms with which so formidable a fortress had been taken. Morgan sent him a pistol and ammunition, which he suggested the Governor of Panama should keep for a year, after which he would come and fetch them away. The Governor returned the pistol with a gold ring, warning him 'not to give himself the trouble of coming to Panama because he would not speed so well there as he had sped at Porto Bello'. Plate 4 shows the best sort of pistol used at that period. Actually Morgan waited two years before making his highly successful attack on Panama, after a difficult nine-day journey across the Isthmus; yet even after such a journey the city was taken, with small arms used so effectively as to defeat the fully armed and trained regular Spanish garrison.

Musket-like firelocks and flintlock guns were often carried, and these were used against important human targets in ships such as the gunners or helmsman, just before a boarding party went into action.

Until that lethal weapon the cutlass was fashioned from the hunting machete by the early buccaneers, it can be supposed that any weapons popular at the time for ordinary hand-to-hand fighting were used. Once the design and method of using the cutlass became standardised it superseded all other edged weapons. It is interesting to note that an Englishman, Henry Holland, describing his travels about the Aegean in the early years of the 19th century, mentions how the pirates still to be found in open boats in the approaches to Salonica were armed with pistols and cutlasses.

As a defence against boarders most merchantmen had swivel guns fitted on deck, but once they were discharged there was no time to reload before their gunners were overpowered. Another device used against boarders was the powder chest. This was a small box, about 30cm. by 46cm. and 25-30cm. high, filled with gunpowder, old nails and iron splinters. They were nailed on deck in vulnerable places, such as the poop and on the bulkhead of the waist. From these boxes fuse trains of gunpowder were laid to sheltered positions, from which they could be fired off at will. Despite such devices it is evident that most crews quickly surrendered, despite knowing what their fate as prisoners was likely to be.

To be successful far from home a good ship was needed. To be suitable she had to be reasonably fast and handy, and not too cluttered up with the tophamper and deck houses, so long a characteristic of Continental ships. Even many ships built overseas, both in the New World and the Far East, conformed to Continental practice, with much tophamper which restricted their manoeuvrability. Prizes in the New World which could be regarded as suitable, after alterations, were taken to isolated islands or regular lairs, where necessary modifications could be made. While such alterations to a ship on some remote beach must have been a formidable task it was quite practicable. It must be appreciated that shipbuilding in those days was very different from what it is today. Work was done by hand in the open, and the tools used were of the simplest kind; overseas, dried rays might be used as carpenters' rasps. Plate 5 shows the kind of tools used by the shipwrights and carpenters. This contemporary illustration (1675), believed to be unique, is in *Doctrine of Naval Architecture*, by Sir Anthony Dean, a book in the Pepys Library in Cambridge.

One of the most remarkable pieces of 'do-it-yourself' alterations to a ship was done by Captain Davis to *La Trinidad*, captured off the coast of Peru. Much of this work was done by Spanish carpenters he had taken prisoner, but who were willing to work for 'los diabile Inglese' rather than be executed. In this ship, renamed *Batchelor's Delight*, Captain Davis subsequently circumnavigated South America in 1689: in the Southern Ocean he sighted the Antarctic ice from 63deg. S., the highest latitude reached until a hundred years later when Captain Cook, on his second Pacific voyage, reached 71deg. S.

There were various ways to obtain a ship. A gang in the Caribbean might travel overland to an anchorage where an unsuspecting merchantman could be seized. More remarkable were the attacks made on ships at sea by men who possessed nothing more than ships' boats or canoes. To pass the time in these open boats while waiting the men used to sleep or sing, and these incompatible occupations often led to trouble. No one can know what the songs were about, but since we do know how they occupied their time between voyages it can be imagined that the songs would be unprintable. One unprintable song sometimes heard today originates, so I have been told, from Stuart times.

Since the average ship rarely exceeded five knots, it cannot have been very difficult to get alongside and make fast to a prize, assuming the boats were not sunk by gunfire in the process; this calamity would be avoided by keeping bows-on. Naval guns, whether in men-of-war or merchantmen, could not be depressed very much; consequently, when small boats were used, the nearer to a ship the safer they were.

Piecing together various contemporary accounts of attacks made from boats, in the Caribbean and elsewhere, it is possible to obtain an idea of what actually happened. The pirates were individually armed with smooth-bore pistols and cutlasses. Having worked in close to their ship victim, they threw grapnels to make fast, usually at the stern, up which they swarmed in the face of fierce opposition. After the initial volley the defenders had no time to reload before the hand-to-hand fighting started, in which their opponents were so skilled. Once the attackers were properly on deck they were masters of the situation. They appear to have sustained remarkably few casualties; in fact, they had a saying that many of them were pistol-proof, an expression later used by Shakespeare in 2 Henry IV, 3. In some ways this is understandable because so many pistols were heavy and inaccurate except at close range; the average merchant seaman was unlikely to be a very good shot anyway, as it was a skill only acquired by ceaseless practice. Constant practice with handy pistols and small arms was a feature of pirate life and there are frequent references to it, thus explaining why they were so successful against armed opponents.

When operating with an ordinary ocean-going ship a highly specialised and successful form of attack was used. Despite their lack of discipline there is no doubt that the majority of pirates were excellent seamen; so, when they wanted to, they could sail a ship well and make use of navigational aids, such as rigging stunsails, to obtain extra speed. They used their manoeuvrability and speed to bear down on a collision course towards their opponent, until their bowsprit over-reached the hinder part of the other ship. Once the bowsprit, which was fully manned, was in position, a number of smoke-bombs were thrown down.

These bombs were made of readily combustible materials impregnated with tar and sulphur to produce a suffocating smoke. Into the confusion caused on deck by the bombs, the attackers jumped and let themselves go with dire effect on their opponents from pistols and cutlasses. After what was tantamount to a collision the pirate ship must, on occasions, have sustained some damage; there was also the likelihood of damage due to the ocean swell once the vessels were more or less locked together. I have never seen mention of damage under these circumstances, the risk of which must have been accepted. All wooden ships sustained gale damage so frequently that carpenters were fully accustomed to effecting any kind of repair, all of which could be done by hand.

After taking a prize, and the crew and any passengers had been dealt with, the ship was looted. Most merchantmen were so clumsy as to be of no further use and were just burnt. However, if a particular ship were of a handy type and seemed capable for adaption as a future pirate vessel, she would be manned by a prize crew, together with any 'volunteers' willing to join them; so another raider started her career. When it was decided to burn a captured ship the job was entrusted to the ship's boys, who were suitably rewarded. This could be a hazardous task, because the fire needed to be started well to leeward of their own ship, and the boys often had a long row against the wind and sea back to safety.

There was never much shortage of ships' stores, such as rope or canvas, because these were obtained from captured ships. If necessary, ropes could be made in various parts of the world on the spot from locally-grown fibrous material, which served well in the absence of hemp. Obtaining new masts and spars was always difficult, because few suitable trees from which to make them grow outside the temperate zones. Any particular place where these suitable trees could be obtained was carefully noted, but this source of supply was uncertain and eventually the local scarcity became very acute for everybody. The French actually shipped firs from Europe for use overseas in their men-of-war.

The total number of men in a gang depended to some extent on the size of their ship, but an average crew was anything from one to two hundred. Any discomforts at sea due to overcrowding must have counted for nothing; one two-masted sloop, for instance, had two hundred men on board. Despite overcrowding, which was only for short periods, the ordinary standard of living at sea must in many respects have been as good as in any ocean-going ship of the time. When things were going well the men had their pick of victuals from prizes, together with extras like chocolate and plenty of brandy and wine, though wine was never favoured by any seaman. Rum is always supposed to have been a favourite drink, an idea springing perhaps from the 'Yo, ho, ho, and a bottle of rum'. In fact the production of rum in quantity did not start in the West Indies until the middle of the 17th century, and after it became available brandy was preferred. If supplies of spirit ran short these were eked out by making punch. When a ship touched at any settlement which might be short of liquor, the folk ashore were usually supplied with punch so as not to reduce unduly the ship's liquor supply. Pirates were usually willing to oblige shore settlers in this manner because reasonably good relations ashore anywhere served their interests best in the long run.

Another thing which must have helped good living was the way forays were made ashore, particularly in such regions as the New World and in Madagascar, in order to obtain fresh meat and local foods. These thefts appear to have been accepted by the local inhabitants as a fact of life In the New World the Indian cooks, often carried, were highly skilled as fishermen and also at spearing sea-cows, which provided variety in diet. The tusks of sea-cows, incidentally, were good material from which to make dice. Dice was the popular game at which fortunes were made, and lost, too. Many of the New World Indians in ships, often spoken of as Mosquitomen, possessed astonishing eyesight which made them additionally welcome. They could see and identify a distant sail when it was only just visible to an European using a glass. While the Indians would assist any European who was not a Spaniard, they always preferred the English.

Apart from the escaped slaves on board, who often served in regular capacities in a crew, it was not unusual for sailors to own a slave as a personal servant. Slaves were easy to obtain, and many must have preferred to escape from tyrants ashore for a more dangerous, but probably more humane, existence afloat; it was possible for them even to serve as captain's steward, or in the cook-room, as the galley was then called.

It has been made clear that most captains only exercised proper authority at the time a gang was going into action. There were a few exceptions to this when some captains exerted continual influence by sheer force of personality which, as might be expected, greatly enhanced successes. That highly successful captain, Bartholomew Roberts, was able to enforce a rule in his ship that there should be no gambling and that no women were allowed on board. He must have had a strong character.

While there was little in the way of organised chain of command, a man termed the quartermaster acted as a sort of liaison officer between the captain and the crew in a ship. He would not necessarily succeed to command should anything happen to the captain; there was always another election. Times were when there could be a division of opinion concerning who should be a new captain; then the minority group might leave with their candidate and start up on their own. The experience of many seamen was good, though the majority were unable to apply it to advantage; those that could apply their experience became the natural leaders and head the ruthless gangs which existed.

From Captain Snelgrave's personal account of life in a ship in which he was held prisoner (see Chapter XI), it is evident that a pirate quartermaster was an important person, but, as far as I know, such application of the word quartermaster was not made until the 17th century. We also know from Captain Snelgrave that there was a bos'un, recognised as such, who was the chief petty officer in any ship and responsible for her rigging. Every pirate ship had to care for its gear even if the bos'un possessed only limited authority. Originally, in ordinary ships, the bos'un was known as the counter master (i.e., aft deck master) or master's mate before the latter developed into a rank of its own. In time the duties of proper quartermasters became mainly that of helmsman. When it is remembered that words were spelt phonetically, if written at all, until Dr. Johnson produced his *Dictionary* (1749), it is easy to imagine how counter master could be rendered as quarter master, and so on, the more so because local dialects influenced pronunciation.[1] That attempts were made to preserve some degree of order in certain ships is apparent from the fact that one, a 15th-century Cornish pirate, had four contro (i.e., counter) masters.[2]

The carpenter (a petty officer) in any ship has always been, and still is, a man of almost equal importance to the bos'un, since he is responsible for the hull. The carpenter is necessarily a skilled tradesman, and from the records it is evident that any gang recognised this; though, as explained in the next chapter, he did not get a full cut of a shareout because he was not at much personal risk on board.

From the wrappers of some books it could be imagined that the clothing worn was neat and colourful, topped off with a bandana handkerchief. The garb of the early buccaneers is described in Chapter XII, but judging from later contemporary pictures of pirates some at least were attired in the rather dull Spanish clothing of the period, probably captured. This consisted of a sort of jerkin surmounting a pair of knickerbockers resembling 'plus-fours'. With many large prosperous Spanish towns and settlements in the New World such clothing could be made locally. The material used was a woollen Peruvian product known as Quito cloth, but it was regarded as being somewhat coarse and only suitable for use by colonists of moderate means. The indications are that always there tended to be a local clothing shortage in the Americas, and much clothing came from Europe. Plate 6 shows the dress of an ordinary

17th-century English sailor. While pirates in full commission at sea were able to take what they needed in the way of clothes there were many occasions during expeditions ashore when their clothing problem was acute. One party which travelled back across Darien after various adventures in the Pacific all finished up naked with their bodies painted by friendly Indians. After they boarded a ship on the Atlantic coast it took several months for the dyed skin to resume its proper hue.[3]

Notes

1. Much of the foregoing was explained to me 50 years ago by a retired sailing-ship master.
2. *Miscellaneous Inquisitions.* C145/323. No. 6.
3. Wafer, *loc. cit.*

CHAPTER X

THE SHAREOUT AND OTHER CUSTOMS

THE EARLIEST MENTION of shareouts of which I am
aware occurs in the *Odyssey,* where we learn how spoils
were equally divided among a crew. According to a
Frenchman named Berard who was in the Eastern Mediterranean in the 17th century this system of spoil division still
obtained, except among the corsairs. The crew of a corsair
galley got nothing, being regarded as expendable by the
fighting men; the only food the unfortunate galley slaves
ever got was bread, occasionally sardines, and food no one
else on board would touch. During the Viking raids in
Northern Europe all loot was placed in a common pool and
divided up under rules resembling those at a later date,
which took into account the contributions made by various
members of a gang to the success of an enterprise. As with
other pirates, Viking loot became the personal property of
individuals; Vikings were never accountable in any way to
their home governments.

The system of shareouts used in Elizabethan and subsequent times was really a misapplication in practice of the
Laws of Oléron, which for several years regulated the
payment of seamen. Seaman used not to be paid on a
flat-rate scale, because often they had a lading of goods of
their own among the cargo of the ship in which they were
serving. 'Sirs, will you freight your rates, or will you hire
yourselves according to the freight of the ship?' This offer
occurs in the Laws enacted in the reign of Richard II
(1377-1399), which established the principle that sailors'
pay was linked with voyage profits, and that crews were
recognised almost to be partners in ventures in which the

attendant hazards were shared by everyone. Until the demise of organised piracy everything captured was pooled, and woe betide anyone who so failed to contribute. The penalty for the offender was either to be shot out of hand, or else to be put ashore on some uninhabited island, possibly with a musket, and left to fend for himself. Over the years there are several accounts of how a ship had visited some remote island by chance, there to discover human skeletons. Sometimes it was sadly obvious that these were of the survivors from shipwreck; at other times there was a different explanation.

One system of sharing in the New World was based on the Spanish coin, the piece of eight (eight reales). The share on each 'round' was captain 500, surgeon 250, men 200, and carpenter 150. Although the surgeon was usually paid a fee of about 200 dollars a voyage, presumably from general funds, in addition he received a share of booty. The carpenter, an important man in any ship, went short because he was regarded as not incurring much personal risk.

Another system worked like this. After calculations about the value of the prize and the number to share it, the captain had five times a seaman's share, the mate or quartermaster twice that of a seaman, and the boys half a share. Any residue was then equally divided. After a real success it was not unusual for a seaman's share to be worth 5,000 pieces of eight, i.e., well over £1,000 in those days, and ten times as much today. Either system of sharing would suggest that the captain's share was not over-generous; still it must be remembered that a captain was only really a captain in the accepted sense when attacks were being planned or made. Any slaves on board usually were given a cut of 100 pieces of eight each.

An unwritten rule of the Brotherhood of the Main in the New World concerned hesitancy: on one occasion during a single boat attack on a ship in the open sea, the leader considered that there was some reluctance by his men to press on with the assault, so he knocked holes in the bottom of their boat. When some awkward question arose in America about which a decision had to be taken, the convenient phrase often used was 'that it was not the custom of the coast'.

With all their evil they had a remarkable sense of fairness. Although the Spaniards were their traditional sworn enemies for two centuries, the Brotherhood felt very strongly about the merciless way they had always treated the local Indians. In places where this treatment of the Indians was known to have been particularly bad the Spaniards got no quarter at all, and were freely subjected to the tortures, mostly originated by the Inquisition, they had used on the helpless Indians. All this had a long-term result as many of the successes ashore were due to Indian help.

Despite the fact that the membership of gangs often changed due to casualties or disagreements, there was a striking cameraderie among them, and it is remarkable how the wounded were cared for and a well-paid surgeon made available whenever possible. Apart from the understandable desire of any group of men in hazardous occupations to have medical aid available, there was a very special reason for any sailors involved in fighting afloat to have a surgeon on board. Just as after battles ashore in those it was common practice for obviously fatally-wounded soldiers to be put out of their misery, so at sea similar casualties were often thrown overboard when there was no surgeon available. To put shipmates over the side must have been a very distasteful decision for those having to make it. When there was a surgeon it is unlikely that any effort was spared to do something for serious casualties even with meagre equipment and facilities; while there is life there is hope, however slender it may be. Some men must have sustained grievous wounds bravely borne. It is told how a Captain Taws had the rim of his pelvis carried away and was seen holding his bowels in his hands, but no one could do anything for him.

There was a practice in most ships that if a man were buried at sea under ordinary circumstances the committal was marked by firing volleys. These were called French volleys; there were also English volleys, but how many shots were in these is not recorded. Dampier often mentions the way this reverence was observed by pirates and privateers.

Long after the real significance of Elizabethan religious fervour was forgotten, it lingered on in the practice of some gangs preceding a raid with a Divine Service; on its successful conclusion another of Thanksgiving would be held. While such services were taking place anyone who interrupted was liable to be shot.

The nursing care given to sick companions by these rough men put to shame the comparative neglect of many seamen leading legitimate lives, particularly in the navy. Until the reforms in the naval service introduced by Lind, Trotter and Blane, those celebrated 18th-century surgeons, anything in the way of an invalid diet was barely thought about; in fact if a seaman stricken with a fever could not face ordinary ship's food there was nothing else to give him unless it came from the table of a sympathetic captain. Pirates in the Caribbean often had Indian cooks who could devise for invalids various pulses, and also broths made from sea cows and iguanas.

Among the early buccaneers from Tortuga there was a recognised scale of payments for serious injuries, very reminiscent of payments by insurance companies in modern times under accident policies. The scale was as follows:

For the loss of a hand, arm, leg or foot	£26
For an eye, a finger or a toe	£13
Daily subsistence allowance, up to 2 months ..	12½p

If by any chance an attack had not provided sufficient loot for a proper pay-out another one was immediately undertaken to make up the deficiency. Whether the foregoing systems of shareouts and 'accident insurances' were used later by the highly organised Madagascar pirates I have not seen recorded.

Just because we happen to know so much about the sordid life of the latter-day, and often wealthy, pirates, it does not follow that others of the same persuasion in earlier centuries behaved differently. In their relationships with each other they must have had established codes of conduct, conformity to which was necessary to make life tolerable for groups of ruthless men living at close quarters. It is also obvious that the quantities of loot often to be shared out could inevitably give rise to lots of trouble unless a strictly enforced sharing rule existed. All the other rules, more domestic in character, mentioned earlier had been shown by experience to be needed.

In the Middle Ages and in Elizabethan times the temptations of the flesh on offer in English and other European ports never approached conditions in the places overseas, later frequented by seamen of all nationalities. Although for limited periods pirates lived hard, many were able to compensate for it between voyages by luxurious living in a manner no ordinary seamen could ever hope to equal. So just to become a pirate opened up vistas of wealth beyond belief, and simple illiterate men who took the plunge often came into possession of thousands of pounds sterling. Most or all of this was lost gambling or by local debauchery. Some, more provident men, buried their treasure in the expectation that they could return to their cache at some future time. How many lived to do this is unknown, but there cannot have been many who survived long enough to do so; many a tale has been based on buried treasure of this nature. Few ever returned home as rich men, if they reached home at all. If they did there was always the chance that they might be blackmailed if someone recognised them; if they were exposed it meant conviction and hanging. John Avery (born 1665) of Plymouth, a notorious Madagascar pirate, was one such who returned to England and settled in Bideford with a store of wealth in the form of jewels. To obtain cash by sale of these he made periodic journeys to Bristol, where, after a time, suspicions were aroused and he became the victim of blackmail which finally rendered him penniless. Yet in just one (Indian owned) ship he took no less than 100,000 pieces of eight. What an end to a man who once upon a time had been the respected mate of a merchantman!

Just when the skull and crossbones became the distinctive flag is unknown, but in England during the early 17th century this emblem was increasingly used symbolically in churchyards and similar places where there was emphasis on death. Since there is no reference to the use of skull and crossbones at sea until the 17th century, it is quite likely that the device was adopted for the same reason that it was used in the churchyards. The crossbones flag took two forms; there was either the simple one, or the more elaborate type portraying a skeleton with a dagger in one hand and a rummer—a special kind of wine-glass—in the other. This particular glass (Plate 7) came into use in England in the later 17th and early 18th century, mainly in taverns, to serve the various rum concoctions then becoming popular. Presumably some of these glasses may have reached the New World to be copied on a flag, but glass drinking-vessels in any ship in those days were scarce due to ordinary maritime hazards; pewter mugs, drinking horns, and even coconut shells were often used, except in first-class ships like the East Indiamen. Cargoes of all manner of domestic utensils were shipped to the American colonists, and pirates would fit themselves out from captures. At this time much wine was exported from Europe, and white wine production was rapidly developing in the Rhine and Mosel valleys. These new wines became popular in Western Europe and to some extent in England. To serve them a new kind of wine-glass was made in quantity, soon becoming widely available. These glasses were called römers, but a contemporary rendering of the name was rummers, understandable in the days of phonetic spelling. Since these glasses were so popular it is likely that stocks were sent across the Atlantic; so a reproduction might have appeared on flags. If any römers got into the hands of pirates they would hardly be used for wine, rarely drunk unless there was nothing else available, since brandy was the sailor's favourite drink at sea; rum was less popular. Still, most people would agree that a drink of any kind tastes better, or at least is more attractive, when served in a glass instead of a mug or a coconut shell. As can be seen from the illustration, the tavern rummer had such a distinctive shape that it was probably the glass reproduced on a flag and not the more common römer. Since no flag has survived the whole matter must remain an interesting speculation. Captain Johnson (*loc. cit.*), writing in 1715, mentions a rummer (spelt thus) being incorporated in a pirate flag, which may have been at the whim of a captain who happened to have some glasses in his ship.

At the peak of the great privateer/pirate activities around 1680 certain captains flew what might be called their personal house flags. Dampier mentions various captains he met at the time who did this. Sharp had red and green with white ribbons, Hawkins had red striped with yellow, Coxon had plain red, and Harris plain green. Later, in Madagascar, a Captain Nissen had his own flag but no record of its design survives. The wearing of a special flag can hardly be called an idiosyncrasy; but the Earl of Cumberland (1558–1605) who made 12 voyages could always be identified at sea by the immaculate way he dressed, even to the extent of carrying gloves. He is better known perhaps for his successful capture of San Juan, Puerto Rico, in 1598, after both Drake and Hawkins had been unable to do this, mainly because so many of their men were stricken down with yellow fever. Even so, owing to its situation and layout, San Juan would have been difficult to take at the best of times.

After ocean-going ships came into general use in the latter part of the 17th and during the 18th century, when they met at sea, pirate captains used to salute each other with guns. Often these might be loaded with ball ready for other purposes, but no matter! In many ships there was much carelessness with weapons of all kinds, and even gunpowder might not get the respect it deserved; men would sustain nasty burns from spilt powder. Apart from such accidents magazines would explode with the loss of the ship under the sort of circumstances described in the next chapter.

CHAPTER XI

THE EXPERIENCES OF TWO SHIPMASTERS

IT HAS BEEN MADE OBVIOUS that the passengers or crew of any ship captured were in for a very bad time, often fatal. While the nature of horrors that might be experienced can be gathered from various sources, the atrocities practised on any particular occasion were simply at the whim of the captors. It is understandable that fully detailed accounts of events after a ship was taken are scarce; few escaped to tell the tale anyway, and those who survived their experiences were probably not very anxious to record them even if they had literary inclinations.

However, authentic accounts[1] of two incidents in the early 18th century narrated by the shipmasters involved who managed to escape reveal what must have been experienced by many others less fortunate. Captain Mackray who just escaped with his life after the capture of *Triton*, East Indiaman (see page 160), was at least spared the abuse and cruelties experienced by Captain Snelgrave in 1718, and Captain Roberts three years later.

Captain Snelgrave's *Bird*, a large London ship, loaded in Holland for the Guinea Coast, where she would pick up a cargo of slaves for America, the first stage of the triangular run common in those days. On the West African coast she anchored in a Sierra Leone river where three vessels were lying, which turned out to be pirates; between them they had already taken 10 English ships.

It was about eight o'clock in the evening when a boat was heard rowing towards *Bird*. At the sound of oars, the mate, named Jones, was ordered to send 20 armed men on the deck to be prepared in case the strange boat should prove hostile. The reply to a hail was, '*The Two Friends,* of Barbados, Captain Elliott'. The boat was hailed a second time, with the reply that they were from America; this was accompanied with a volley of small arms. Captain Snelgrave now told Jones to return the fire, which was not done as his mate reported that the crew refused to obey orders. Only later it was discovered that Jones himself had prevented the men from firing, having previously been in communication with the pirates.

So the boat came alongside the ship unopposed; *Bird* was boarded and a volley immediately fired into the steerage, mortally wounding a sailor; at this the crew asked for quarter, which was granted. The leader of the boarding party, named Cocklyn, then demanded of Captain Snelgrave why he had dared to order his men to fire at them: he explained that it was his duty to defend his ship. Cocklyn pressed a pistol at the Captain's chest, which he was able to parry before it went off, the ball passing between his side and arm; he was then struck with the butt end of the pistol, which knocked him down, but, quickly recovering himself, Snelgrave ran up on deck. There he encountered the bos'un who cut at him with a broadsword, declaring that no quarter should be given to him because he attempted to defend his vessel. He evaded the blow by stooping below the quarterdeck rail, into which it cut for an inch, breaking the sword. The man then took a pistol, some of which were heavy weapons in those days, and was about to beat out his brains, but was restrained by the others. But they then immediately turned upon the crew of *Bird* whom they cut and maimed terribly, despite the fact that they had surrendered. Cocklyn now came on deck and ordered the hands of *Bird's* crew to be tied, telling the captain his life was safe if none of his own crew had any complaints to make against him, which Snelgrave thought unlikely, as he had given them no cause.

At this stage several volleys of small-arms were fired to signal the capture of a prize, and orders were given to prepare a large celebration meal on board. Most merchantmen on long voyages carried livestock to supplement the unattractive preserved food, and the heads of the fowls, ducks,

geese and turkeys available were simply cut off and
wing feathers drawn; no one would wait for proper plucking.
The birds were flung as they were into the large coppers
provided to cook the meals for 500 negroes due to be loaded
on the Guinea Coast. Several hams were added, with a large
in-pig sow, and the ship's cook was told to boil the lot together;
meanwhile the surgeon was allowed to dress the wounded.

Shortly afterwards the pirate quartermaster asked the
time by Captain Snelgrave's watch, which Snelgrave
produced, saying it was a very good gold-cased one, the kind
that would be treasured by any real seaman. The quartermaster merely held it up by the chain, and then laying it on
the deck, gave it a kick, remarking that it made a good
football. At this someone picked it up and put it in a
common chest, like the other loot, before the mast.

Captain Snelgrave was then taken on board a pirate ship
lying a short distance away, where he was asked details about
Bird and her sailing qualities. After explaining these he was
told she would serve their purpose admirably. Soon after
he was taken on board this other vessel, a well-armed man
came up, saying that his name was Jack Griffin, one of his
old schoolfellows. Since Captain Snelgrave did not appear
to recollect him, he mentioned various pranks played
together in their youth. He explained that he had been
mate of an English vessel, but had been forced into pirate
service to act as master of a crew he described as a most
atrocious lot. Griffin promised to ensure Snelgrave's safety,
as everybody would soon get intoxicated with the liquor
on board their new prize. Griffin obtained a bowl of punch,
and led the way to the cabin where there was simply a carpet
to sit upon, because the ship was always kept cleared for
action. They sat down crossed-legged, and Griffin drank
Snelgrave's health, remarking that his crew had spoken well
of him so he need not fear for his life. Griffin then proposed
a toast to James III, meaning the Old Pretender, which
seemed to indicate that he had been one of his supporters
during the Jacobite Rebellion of 1715.

A hammock was slung for Captain Snelgrave at night,
by the intercession of Griffin, but the others 'lay rough'

so as to be ready for instant action; even their captain was not allowed a bed, faring like the rest. Snelgrave eventually got into his hammock, but could not sleep owing to the loud and characteristically foul conversation around him. Griffin, true to his undertaking to guard his old schoolfellow while asleep, remained nearby, sword in hand. Towards morning, while the pirates were still carousing on deck, the bos'un, intoxicated, came towards the hammock swearing that he would slice Captain Snelgrave for ordering his crew to fire. He dragged him from his hammock, and would, no doubt, have carried out his threat had it not been for Griffin, who, as he pressed forward to stab him, cut at the man with his sword and after a struggle succeeded in beating him off. At length everyone fell asleep and Snelgrave was no longer molested.

Next day Griffin complained about the bos'un's conduct, for which the man was threatened with a flogging; but Snelgrave wisely pleaded for him as he was drunk at the time. That day ten of Captain Snelgrave's men and the mate Jones joined the pirates; in fact, it was obvious that it had been Jones who had made the capture of *Bird* so easy. *Bird* was ransacked and quantities of goods from her cargo, of which no use could be made, were thrown overboard. By the evening, cargo worth three or four thousand pounds had been wasted; money and articles of clothing were the only things the pirates really wanted. For the time being Captain Snelgrave was kept in the pirate ship.

There was then living in Sierra Leone a Captain Glynn, who, despite having suffered at the hands of pirates, was on good terms with them, although he did not collaborate. He was intimate with two of the other captains in the river, one of whom, named Davis, kept his crew strictly disciplined. We first hear about this Captain Davis and the man named Cocklyn (who possibly once held a command) in the Bahamas a year before the event now described. They appear to have left the Bahamas to start operations off the Guinea Coast about the time Captain Woods Rogers was sent from England to Nassau (see page 42). Glynn and Davis went on board the vessel in which Snelgrave

was held prisoner to protest about his ill-usage. In consequence, he was allowed to return to *Bird* where he found
the havoc was irreparable; his desks were broken and robbed,
and even books, utterly useless to others, had been taken
out of chests and flung overboard. He had now to accept the
insult of a shipmaster sitting in his own cabin, and the sight
of those all around consuming his liquors and other good
things from his private store, which, happily, put them into
good humour. Nevertheless, a quarrel started, and those
involved were going back on board their own ships to
prepare to fight it out, but were somehow restrained from
doing so by the intervention of Captain Snelgrave. He then
had another narrow escape from the bos'un who had tried
to attack him in his hammock: the man drew a pistol on
him, which fortunately misfired; but the pirate carpenter,
taking the prisoner's part, beat up his shipmate severely
enough to nearly kill him.

The next day saw further waste of property, and nothing
could be more typical of pirate conduct than what went on.
Half hogsheads of claret[2] and brandy in the cargo were
hoisted on deck, the heads were knocked in and cans and
bowls dipped into them until the men were satisfied; they
then tipped the rest over each other. After the containers
on deck were empty they hoisted up more; and in the
evening washed the deck with what remained. They
demolished the bottled liquors by striking off the necks
with their cutlasses, so that soon only a little brandy
remained of all the ship's stock. The stores of sugar,
butter, and cheese disappeared in this mad riot. A man who
stumbled over a bundle of the captain's necessaries which
he had been allowed to keep, flung it overboard, 'because
it lay that way'.

One man named Kennedy, noticing a packet in which was
a black suit of clothes belonging to the prisoner, picked it
up, together with a good hat and wig. Snelgrave in vain told
him that he had been allowed to retain them, whereupon
Kennedy struck him with the flat of his sword and warned
him never to dispute a pirate's will, and that he might lose
his life for doing so. Kennedy put on the clothes; half-an-hour

afterwards he took them off again and threw them over-board, after others had drenched him with buckets of claret. This particular man who, it is said, was originally a London pickpocket, ended his career at Execution Dock, Wapping.

Soon after all this Captain Snelgrave obtained leave to go ashore to the house of Captain Glynn, where various captains received him civilly, saying that they would do all in their power to recover some of his personal belongings for him. He was now so short of clothes that he was even obliged to borrow a shirt from Captain Glynn, since he had been three days without a change in the hot sticky climate. Eventually the captains went on board *Bird* with their prisoner, and one of them persuaded Cocklyn, obviously an influential man, to address the crew on Snelgrave's behalf. The result was an agreement to give Captain Snelgrave a ship captured earlier which they intended to quit, together with what remained of his own cargo; also, they offered to add a large quantity of goods taken from other prizes but of no use to them. This was a delicate matter, as such goods were the property of various merchants; if found in his possession they would lay Snelgrave himself open to a charge of piracy. After explanations by Davis he was allowed to decline the offer.

The ship they were abandoning was then laid alongside *Bird,* and a considerable portion of the cargo remaining in her was saved and hoisted into the other. Unfortunately, all Snelgrave's trading goods, consisting of cloths, liquors and fine goods, had been destroyed. Pieces of best holland had been unfolded on the deck, on which the pirates had lain down half drunk. Buckets of wine had stained the linen which was then flung into the sea.

After the various negotiations about his future Captain Snelgrave was allowed to sleep in *The Two Friends* and given shore leave when he pleased. On board this ship he slept four nights, until the replacement vessel given him was loaded. During this period, Cocklyn, who had fired at him when *Bird* was first boarded, was attacked with a bad fever and asked to see him alone, begging forgiveness. He also ordered his boy to give Captain Snelgrave the key of his sea chest, and to let him take anything he wanted, a chance Snelgrave did not hesitate to take since he was so badly in need of clothing. Later, Cocklyn became delirious and died the same night, cursing his Maker in such a frightful manner that it influenced several men new to the game privately to ask Captain Snelgrave's advice about how they might quit. Since a proclamation of pardon had been issued in September 1717 (see page 41) to all who surrendered, they were advised to avail themselves of this opportunity.

Three laced coats among the plunder from *Bird* were the cause of another dispute in which Captain Snelgrave was involved, resulting in a threat by a man named Williams that he should be cut to pieces. This revealed a curious example of pirate vanity: Snelgrave followed previous advice by Captain Elliot and addressed the man as 'captain', so gratifying him that he sent him a keg of wine!

To celebrate the commissioning of *Bird* as a pirate ship, renamed *The Wyndham Galley*, Captain Snelgrave was invited to dine on board, and at the party the stems of toast glasses (Plate 8) were broken, and guns fired. To add to the excitement some cartridges caught fire in the powder room where a scuttle had stupidly been left open during the gunfire; nearby were several tons of gunpowder, which, fortunately, did not ignite. Fires then became almost the order of the day, as the next event was the customary burning of the unwanted ship, *Rising Sun,* which would be replaced by the captured *Bird.* Still events were not yet concluded.

The captain named Davis was always reasonably well disposed towards Snelgrave, so the latter inquired if there were any chance of his obtaining local liberty for the time being. This was granted with an invitation by Davis to supper on board his ship. In the middle of supper, at about eight in the evening, there was a cry of 'fire'. The greater part of the crew were drunk, and there were more than 50 prisoners from various ships confined on board at the time. A fire in any of those wooden ships was always a terrifying business and, in the inevitable confusion, the only thought of the more sober was to get away in the boats; guns had to be fired to make them return. Meanwhile the flames increased rapidly, and spread towards the hold, where there were no less than 15 tons of gunpowder. One man, Taylor, more composed than most in the pandemonium, put his head up the hatchway and shouted for blankets and water, urging that if these were not brought quickly the ship must blow up. Captain Snelgrave caught up all the blankets and rugs he could find, which Taylor placed against the bulkhead of the powder-room and poured water on to them from buckets to prevent them catching fire. The night was dark, the crew mostly drunk; it seemed there was little hope of mastering the fire. To jump overboard was certain death from the sharks hovering around the vessel, so Snelgrave took a quarter-deck grating and lowered it into the sea, hoping to get away upon that, as several men had seized the only boats and made off in them.

While he was thinking about his own escape he heard a shout, 'for a brave blast to go to hell with'. In the general confusion 50 or more of the crew had got on the bowsprit and spritsail yard, in the vain hope that they might escape destruction there. Meanwhile Taylor and the others laboured to subdue the flames in the hold until they succeeded, though they were all badly burned. It appeared that the fire had been started by a negro who had gone with a candle to draw rum, and had set the spirits on fire, together with another cask close by. Fortunately, 20 other casks of rum and as many of tar and pitch had escaped, otherwise the vessel could not have been saved.

The services of Captain Snelgrave that night gained him the respect of all his captors. They sent word to him about their customary sale before the mast, where many bought things which had belonged to him and returned them. He speedily went ashore with his purchases, and was advised to escape into the woods until the coast was clear. When the pirates had left Sierra Leone he returned to Captain Glynn, boarded his substitute ship with all the goods he could find, and sailed for England, with six shipmasters whose vessels had been destroyed and no less than 60 other passengers more fortunate than most under similar circumstances. He arrived in Bristol in August 1719.

What happened to Captain Roberts after being captured provides a striking example of the way human beings can survive extreme privation and hardships. Like Captain Snelgrave he was in the Guinea trade, when his ship was taken near St. Nicholas in the Cape Verde Islands. His captors, realising he was a talented shipmaster, did their utmost to persuade him to join them. One captain in particular treated him with indulgence, and initially he was at least allowed to remain a prisoner in his own ship which, nevertheless, was quickly stripped bare. But this concession did not last long, because at a party to which he had been invited in a pirate ship he refused to drink the health of the Old Pretender (James III). To refuse to drink the toast would normally not be regarded as anything very serious elsewhere at the time, but not so in that ship; one of the captains even threatened to shoot him through the head. It is curious to reflect that this was another occasion when the Old Pretender featured in pirate life; just why this should be so, six years after the Jacobite Rebellion, when George I from Hanover had become king of England, is hard to understand. After being savagely treated Captain Roberts was roughly forced on board his own ship at midnight and turned adrift with no water or stores of any kind, no sails, and no means of even getting a light. With him were two boys, one only eight years old.

Because his ship was leaky the first thing Roberts did was to try and pump her out with the help of the elder boy, a task whick took him until daylight. At dawn the ship was searched, and all that could be found in the way of food was a little stale bread, ten gallons of rum, a little rice and flour, and only two gallons of water. Fortunately some old canvas was found from which, after three days' stitching, Roberts was able to make a sail.

The three on board fed on raw flour and rice and drank rum; this, remember, in a sub-tropical climate. Such a diet soon made them suffer ill effects, and as an alternative they tried making a flour dough with some of the remaining water. A rainstorm relieved their immediate thirst, but they were only able to collect a gallon. However, they husbanded their provisions so well that, with the addition of a shark they caught, the small stock lasted for three weeks, and they were spared inevitable famine by sighting the island of St. Anthony, Cape Verde Islands. Before they could reach the landing place darkness had set in, and they anchored to await daylight. Their thirst had become so severe that the elder boy offered to go ashore in a small boat for water and to return immediately.

No sooner was he gone than Roberts, completely worn out, retired to his cabin and dropped off to sleep. At midnight he woke up and, coming up on deck, found to his alarm that they were dragging their anchor and were already almost out of sight of land. At this latest misfortune he doubted whether he could regain the shore without assistance of the elder boy, while to make matters worse, the ship was making water fast.

The danger of sinking being greatest, Roberts went to the pump and in a few hours got the ship dry. His next task was to get the anchor up, and somehow he succeeded. Parched with thirst, he now managed to get back to the island, and eventually dropped anchor in a sandy bay, where the same evening some negroes came to his assistance, bringing water with them. Encouraged by this, and with some of the other negroes, whose help had been obtained by the boy who remained ashore, he attempted to enter the port of Paraghesi. However, in the night the improvised sail split, which so frightened the negroes that they instantly took to their boat, leaving Captain Roberts still in a pretty hopeless situation.

Next day while he was somehow finding enough strength to steer the ship, he heard voices in the hold and found three negroes, now sobering up, who had been left dead drunk by their companions. These men, giving themselves up for lost when they discovered where they were, at first would render him no assistance, but, later, began to help work the ship. One of them pretended to know the harbour; however, when he approached the entrance he was obviously lost and wanted to run the ship on to some rocks. At this Roberts threatened to despatch anyone who should attempt to do so; immediately the pretending pilot jumped overboard and swam ashore with the other negroes. That evening, in bright moonlight, Captain Roberts saw several natives on the rocks, who in the morning swam out offering any help they could if he would go ashore, where they had made a large fire to welcome him. Unfortunately, he could not swim, so for the present was obliged to remain on board, but the natives made his situation more tolerable by bringing fish and other provisions. Readers may wonder why, despite the current, Roberts's progress into harbour was not better. But ships in those days were lumpy vessels, very sensitive to changes in wind and tide, even with a full crew; and here was a ship under jury rig manned by one man and a young boy, both completely exhausted.

The next day the weather looked threatening and Captain Roberts feared being driven out to sea. The natives again helped and, after trying in vain to fasten a rope to the rocks, offered to swim with him and the boy to land. Unwilling to abandon ship while any hope remained of saving her, he toiled on; but next day, in spite of all his efforts, the weather broke and drove the ship on to rocks which pierced her bottom. The water was now rising rapidly and all the locals left him, but as soon as the weather moderated they returned and rescued the boy, and two of them swam ashore with the captain.

Despite even this, his new situation was alarming. He was stranded on a ledge of rocks, under the cover of others which overhung his head. These rose to a fearsome height, and it was at much danger to themselves that the friendly natives had descended to his assistance. He was too weak to climb, and because he could not swim to a landing place as the locals did, his immediate prospects were not very bright.

On this ledge Roberts and his boy remained for several days, still visited by the natives, who exerted themselves greatly for him. Among those who came was an European, who, to his surprise, spoke to him in English. He explained that he was a Welshman, named Franklin, who had been for some time held prisoner by pirates, but had escaped and managed to reach this island.

Captain Roberts, realising that he was marooned, tried with assistance to scale the overhanging cliff, which was several hundred feet high, but understandably failed. This exertion was the last straw and his health collapsed. For a month he was ill on the rocky ledge, and his survival was mainly due to constant attentions by islanders who had to scale the cliffs for every visit. Finally the only boat of the island somehow managed to reach him and he was rescued.

Then came the problem of how to get away from the island. Nothing daunted by his experiences, Roberts built a boat from flotsam and jetsam timber, in which he reached another of the Cape Verde islands. There he was picked up during the chance visit of an English ship, in which he had further alarming adventures, unrelated to pirates; these delayed him so much that he did not finally reach England until three years after he had started his original voyage.

Notes

1. *See also, Remarkable Voyages and Shipwrecks.* C. W. Barrington. Simpkin Marshall.

2. There was a big demand for claret by the American colonists.

CHAPTER XII

THE BUCCANEER STORY

THIS IS REALLY A STORY beginning on the island of St. Catherine, now called St. Kitts, about men of French origin, though men from most European countries joined them later.

In 1623 two men, D'Esnambue and Thomas Warner (knighted in 1638), partitioned St. Kitts and established French and English settlements there; but six years afterwards the Spaniards invaded the island and drove all the settlers out. Many managed to escape by sea, but the only practicable place to go was to Tortuga, an island off the north-western coast of Hispaniola; this island's name was a corruption from the original, La Espanola, bestowed by Columbus when he discovered it in 1492. In Tortuga the new arrivals were joined by a number of Dutchmen who had been expelled from Santa Cruz (now the U.S.A.-owned island of St. Croix).

After an occupation lasting 100 years, Hispaniola was practically abandoned by the Spaniards early in the 17th century. It had been stripped of its mineral resources, and in just the first 15 years an estimated number of 100,000 Arawak inhabitants were ruthlessly killed. To avoid the onslaught of the Spaniards, both here and in other West Indian islands, thousands of Caribs committed suicide, and even mothers destroyed their babies to save them from the miseries of living. If escaping Caribs were caught they were flogged, or had boiling water or molten lead poured over them.

Some of the Spaniards remaining on Hispaniola turned pirate, confining their attentions to Spanish ships, which they knew were the richest, but the worst-provided and the worst-defended of any nation. The ships used by these Spaniards were engaged ostensibly in the slave trade to supply labour needed by any planters still on Hispaniola. But all this was short-lived, because the planters could not obtain enough slave labour to make their efforts worthwhile and the whole economy and shipping of Hispaniola finally collapsed. Because they were supposed to be slavers the Spanish ships managed to remain immune from the attentions of Spanish men-of-war operating in the Caribbean. The whole affair was a curious incident, and was one of the few occasions when Spanish ships with Spanish crews are known to have engaged in piracy.

Then other Europeans moved in. The French, English and Dutch refugees from St. Kitts who were already on Tortuga started settlements on Hispaniola; they were joined in due course by more Englishmen, who had been attempting to colonise an island off the coast of Central America. An arrangement was made with Dutch shipowners to keep them all supplied with basic necessities in exchange for hides and tallow; this was easy because Hispaniola was well stocked with wild cattle and pigs, and organised hunting began immediately. This informal trading agreement had repercussions later when the French home government and the French West Indian Company started to obtain formal control of the adjacent island of Tortuga. For a long time both tried unsuccessfully to expel the Dutchmen, all of whom were fully accepted as established local inhabitants despite their nationality.

The new settlers became known as *boucaniers* or buccaneers, a name originating in the manner described in Chapter I. Some grew tired of hunting and became planters, while others took to the sea as pirates. To distinguish the pirates from the buccaneers proper, the French called them *flibustiers,* which was often rendered as filibusters. The small boats these men initially used at sea were called fly-boats, a name derived from the part designation 'fil' of those who had them. Most of the early French colonists in the New World and all the French seamen came from north-west

France, and Norman French, frequently Anglicised, was the language widely spoken in the region. In Hispaniola it was a particularly hybrid tongue, mixed up with local words (usually names of objects), this mixture forming the basis for the Creole I have heard spoken in Haiti today.

While settlement on the main island was beginning, the small adjacent one of Tortuga was wholly occupied, and it rapidly prospered both from bucan-making and from planting. The settlers in early days were all men, and by custom they all had assumed names. Later, some of the planters found themselves wives and then their proper names were inserted in the marriage contract. This was the basis of the buccaneer proverb that 'a man is not known until he takes a wife'.

After leaving them unmolested for nine years the Spaniards started again to try and drive from the regions those they regarded as aliens. The island of Tortuga was surprised and everyone there was killed, including all who surrendered in the hope of receiving some clemency.

Having ruthlessly dealt with Tortuga the Spaniards then turned their attention to Hispaniola proper, obviously a more formidable objective. It was only after several years that the buccaneers there were more or less overpowered. Nevertheless, strong-posts held out, and ultimately the French firmly established themselves throughout the hilly part of the island now constituting Haiti, the native name for 'the mountainous land'; the Spaniards confined themselves thereafter to the flatter eastern part.

Survivors from the Spanish onslaught either betook themselves to various small islands, where they were left in peace, or else turned to piracy, which soon became an increasingly important feature of the Caribbean scene.

Tortuga was successfully reoccupied in 1638 by the French and Dutch, and what had hitherto been an agricultural island soon became in important pirate stronghold for a society called the Brethren of the Coast, whose sole purpose was to attack Spanish ships. This successful re-occupation was mainly due to the help and leadership given by an Englishman named Willis. He arrived at an opportune moment with 300 fellow countrymen from Nevis, whence they had been driven by an overwhelming Spanish attack after a further attempt to establish an English settlement there. Willis was a man of unusually forceful character and, after Tortuga was reoccupied, it was under his guidance that the regular organised attacks on Spanish shipping commenced. Apparently Willis somehow fell out with the French, because, later, he left with a number of other Englishmen for St. Kitts, and turned out a party of Frenchmen in occupation there. In 1641 the new and increasingly powerful French Charter Company, Compagnie des Indes, took Tortuga into its orbit: it accepted the fact that the economy of the island was based on piracy and was glad to participate in the ill-gotten gains to be had there. It may be wondered why Englishmen in the West Indies received so little help or encouragement from London, but all the troubles with Charles I and the Civil War in the middle of the 17th century did not permit many ventures overseas.

News spread as to how matters had developed in Hispaniola and Tortuga, and, despite memories of the earlier massacres, many Frenchmen emigrated from Europe to become indentured for three years with either the buccaneers or the planters. So in time there were four classes of inhabitants: the buccaneers proper, the *flibustiers*, the *habitans* or planters, and the *engagés* or indentured youths, all collectively called the Body of Adventurers. For some unknown reason the home government in Paris for a long time took no official interest in these activities.[1]

The general prosperity meant that taverns and bawdy houses soon sprang up where the sea-going buccaneers, or *flibustiers*, were the big spenders. The most notorious houses were in Cayona, the principal town in Tortuga at the time. When they had no more to spend the men went to sea again, very much as happened later on with the patrons of Port Royal, Jamaica, the place where it was remarked, 'there is not now in Port Royal 10 men to every house that selleth liquor'. Dissoluteness reached such a pitch that many wealthy young Frenchmen, anxious for a while to seek adventures in the New World, got themselves entangled in these dives, which was the end of them. Few returned to France to the substantial inheritances often awaiting them.

English pirates always favoured Jamaica as their base for operations because this island had never been permanently occupied by the Spaniards, and it was open to anyone to accept what was termed Jamaica Discipline. Cromwell sent troops under General Venables in 1655 to seize it for England on the advice of Captain William Jackson, himself a pirate, who earlier had made Jamaica his headquarters.

For half a century Tortuga, secure from molestation, was for the buccaneers what Malta was for so long for the Royal Navy.

Every ocean-going ship at that time had to be careened regularly to free her bottom from barnacles and other marine growth. Ships in the New World suffered particularly badly from a local pest called the sucking fish. These fish, about the size of a mackerel, would fasten on to a ship, and a dozen or so could appreciably affect her speed. Careening really corresponded to modern dry-docking, except that the ship was beached and laid right over on her side to permit bottom treatment. Few illustrations of this process exist; Plate 9 shows what it involved. All wooden ships in tropical waters rapidly became fouled, and it was ever a problem trying to keep them clean; but for pirate ships speed was necessary for success, so they were careened frequently. Marine growth was allowed to dry and then burnt and scraped off, a process known as breaming. After this a generous dressing of tallow, or tallow mixed with sulphur, was applied as an anti-fouling agent. In Tortuga, and also in Haiti, the local tidal pattern was particularly favourable for careening. Tallow was cheap and plentiful there, while supplies of sea stores, taken from prizes, could easily be obtained. There were full dockyard facilities, as it would be expressed nowadays, which were increasingly used after the time ocean-going ships replaced the small boats used by the early buccaneers who turned pirate. Because of the generally favourable conditions in the Caribbean for careening, various suitable places were developed later on for the purpose, and French privateers working the Guinea Coast would actually cross the Atlantic, to what was then the French island of St. Lucia, for cleaning and refitting.

It would have been difficult to find a better place for organising piracy than in Tortuga and around the mountainous north-western end of Hispaniola, with its sheltered bays and islands adjacent to the Windward Passage through which most merchant shipping passed. The piracy done from small boats, using the many hidey-holes, was much like the ancient practice in the eastern Mediterranean. The use of proper ships came later as sea-going experience was gained. I was once privileged to imagine for myself on the spot what conditions must have been like nearly three hundred years before.

Considering its importance for so long it is remarkable that so little is known about what Tortuga was like in its heyday, and what went on there. The island (Lat. 20deg. N., Long. 73deg. E.) is 40 kilometres long and about 8 kilometres wide; there is a central hill spine 1,000ft. (305 metres) high, which produces its tortoise-like appearance. The northern Atlantic seaboard is precipitous, but the south coast provides good anchorage and beaches suitable for careening. Here was the harbour of Basse Terre, the chief place for general ship-work, and nearby Cayona, the town notorious for its sleazy excesses. Other places where careening and light repairs were possible are now only fishing villages, with the charming names of Boucan Eulpes, La Vellé and Point-à-Oiseaux. Unfortunately, no good chart of Tortuga exists. With the help of Rear-Admiral Ritchie, C.B., formerly the Naval Hydrographer, the earliest map I have discovered is a sketch-map dated 1650 (Plate 10), and there is also a map showing part of Haiti in an 18th-century French atlas.[2]

Eventually a French governor, Gouverneur des Côtes de St. Domingo, was appointed in the mid-17th century, when his official residence was inland near Palmistre. It was at Palmistre many years later that Pauline Buonaparte Le Clerc (sister of Napoleon), with her husband, General Le Clerc, set up court on high ground to escape malaria and yellow fever. But little remains from those busy bygone days. Along the coast relics such as old guns are occasionally visible through the clear water, while inland overgrown ruins provide tattered memorials to the past.

After this successful occupation of Tortuga there was easy communication with the nearby opposite coast of Hispaniola, where Port de Paix and Cap Francois (now called Cap Haitien) were established in about 1640, and kept free from Spanish interference. Originally these places were used as trading ports by buccaneer hunters, but later they were freely used as pirate bases and provided entertainment similar to that of Cayona for men during their spells ashore. Cap Francois was particularly useful as a port, because the anchorage was protected by two reefs and the entry channels could be defended easily against unwelcome visitors. There is mention in some books of Port au Prince, now the capital of Haiti, being used as a pirate lair. It is quite possible that the sheltered waters around may have been used occasionally; but Port au Prince, as known today, was not founded until 1749, well after the time piracy had ceased in the Caribbean.

For a very long time the buccaneers, the more so after they dominated the pirate scene, had a local way of life most evident in the seaside settlements. There were plenty of negro women about, but they were basically slaves whose importation into Hispaniola by the Spanish had begun as early as 1510. There were half-caste women ready to staff the dives, but it seems they were not particularly popular, at least at the time we are speaking of. In some respects delicacies of feeling, if such existed, are hard to understand; European planters anywhere, even when married, used their own black slave women at will. The progeny of female slaves always belonged to their owner, but on many plantations rearing children was not favoured, because in early days it was considered cheaper to buy replacement slaves from dealers. About 10,000 slaves were imported annually into Hispaniola. When the price of imported slaves rose too high some plantation owners in the West Indies established stud-farms for slave-breeding; in fact, one group of English owners used the island of Barbuda for this purpose, and selected human breeding stock was drafted there. Still, half-caste girls, who somehow lived to grow up, may have escaped to adopt a life very different from that on plantations and certainly very lucrative whenever buccaneers were on a spree.

When Bertrand d'Ogeron was appointed the French governor of Tortuga in 1663 he knew all about this business with women, because he had been a prominent buccaneer himself. One of his first acts was to import 50 'orphans' from France, in much the same way that, earlier, Cromwell sent Irish women to Jamaica. His original appointment as governor was authorised by Cardinal Richelieu with considerable perspicacity, so it is likely that the celebrated cleric knew about d'Ogeron's action, which was covered up at the time by alleging it to be a way of lessening black and white marriages. That this explanation was a trifle weak is revealed by the fact that when the 'orphans' arrived in Tortuga they were sold by public auction! The sale contract included this revealing paragraph: 'I take thee without knowing, or caring to know, who thou art. If anybody from whence thou comest would have thee, thou wouldest not have come in quest of me. But no matter, I do not desire an account of thy past conduct, because I have no right to be offended at it at the time when thou wast at liberty to live ill or well according to thine pleasure, and because I shall have no reason to be ashamed of anything thou wast guilty of when thou didst not belong to me. Give me only thy word for the future, I acquit thee of the past'.

The resident European population of Tortuga in 1664 was about four hundred, to which must be added the number of plantation slaves, half-castes, and the large floating population of seamen; so the habitable parts must have been pretty busy.

When the buccaneers first took to the sea they operated in groups of anything from fifty to one hundred and fifty men, crowded into their open boats of various sizes in which it was barely possible to lie down. Piraguas, originally native canoes, called the flyboats, were used. In these the buccaneers were exposed day and night for a week or more in the open sea, waiting to pounce on ships in or near the

Windward Passage between Cuba and Hispaniola. Probably
the first local man to demonstrate, about 1655, what could
be achieved with simple equipment was named Pierre le
Grand. With an open boat and 28 men he surprised and
captured the ship of the Vice-admiral of the passing Spanish
treasure fleet. After landing the prisoners the Tortugans
successfully sailed their prize to France. When a sturdy
former ship's longboat could be used, it was sometimes
fitted in the bows with a 'pederero' (or 'pateraro'). This
was a swivel gun, in which stones were used as projectiles
instead of proper round shot.

The captain only had authority when the buccaneers were
in action; so inevitably they lived at sea in permanent confusion. There were no proper victualling arrangements, and
often they suffered severe hunger and thirst which made
them even more fierce in action than they were when starting
out. It was only by securing a prize after a long wait that
they knew they could survive at all, an added inducement
to action when a ship appeared. Many who could not find a
prize undoubtedly perished. There were no deliberations
about how to arrange attacks, since the only thing was to
board their opponent quickly. Because their boats were so
small they were able to go in under the guns of any ship,
and as soon as their small-arms were in range they used their
skill picking off anyone at all exposed. At sea firearms and
powder flasks were kept dry by the liberal use of tallow.
Small-arms were always concentrated in the bows of the
boat, which were kept bows-on to target and so less vulnerable to any fire from their opponent. One boat, if there were
several in a given attack, might get in under the stern of a
ship to damage or wedge her rudder. But the main ploy was
to throw out grapnels; directly these held, any ship was as
good as taken. A small point about the handling of these
boards was noticed by Dampier. The oars were always
worked in straps made from manatee (sea cow) hide, and
not in the tholes generally used elsewhere; unfortunately
no reason is given for the practice. In cases of necessity the
ship of any nation would be attacked, but for a long time
the Spanish were the targets of choice. The buccaneers

could thereby seek their vengeance on the people belonging to a nation through which they had all suffered so much, not only in past massacres, but also by depriving them of their hunting which had provided their original means of livelihood.

Outward-bound ships were not favoured, owing to the nature of their cargoes of general merchandise; it was the European-bound treasure ships which they wanted. If ships were in a convoy they would follow them for as much as 100 miles, even as far as the Bahamas, on the off-chance of catching a straggler.

The weapons originally used by the buccaneers for hunting animals were adapted for use at sea to hunt human beings. Their flintlock guns had barrels 138cm. long which fired a ball weighing 28gms.; later, more convenient guns were developed or captured from prize ships. In their hunting days all were first-class shots; they had to be, because if they did not kill a wild bovine, or that dangerous animal the wild boar, with their first (and only) shot, they could easily be killed themselves. This emphasis on good marksmanship continued at sea, where there was frequent practice with small-arms.

The buccaneers' skill with edged weapons such as knives and the machete, really a short sabre, also dated from hunting days when these were in regular use, not only for self-defence, but also to dispose of some quarry which might have been tracked for a long distance. The nature of their life made them fit men; indeed, they had to be fit to travel, on foot, the distances they covered in difficult country, and to manhandle the 27-kilo loads in which hides and meat were packed.

I have seen it stated that the pirate cutlass was the weapon from which the machete, still widely used in Central America, was evolved. All the evidence is that the original hunting machete ultimately became that lethal weapon, the pirate cutlass. Plate 11 shows an early new World hunting knife, no less than 42cms. long, generally of the shape used by the buccaneers and later by pirates.

The dress of buccaneers ashore consisted of shirt and trousers and a pair of hogskin shoes made in one piece.

At sea they went barefooted. Their trousers were held up by a belt from which knives, and, later, a pair of pistols, were suspended. Plate 4 shows an example of a typical northern French pistol (*c.* 1645) of the type mostly used.

Their hat rather resembled a modern hunting cap, with a long peak but no brim. This almost contemporary description of buccaneer attire is at variance with that shown in the few illustrations of the Caribbean pirates at a later period showing them dressed in European-style clothing, possibly due to their use of clothes found in prizes (as mentioned in the previous chapter).

Successful methods of attack originally evolved by the buccaneers were gradually adopted by pirates throughout the world, and in the New World the word buccaneer was eventually used indiscriminately to describe men who had never had any contact with Tortuga.

As time passed the buccaneers learnt more about the sea and were able to use ocean-going ships, in which to extend the scope of their operations far beyond what was possible with small craft sneaking out from places near the Windward Channel. What might be called the small-boat method of attack was not given up entirely, because it still provided a cheap and convenient way for fresh gangs to get started all over the Caribbean. Ordinary ships, in pirate use everywhere by the second half of the 17th century, always favoured Tortuga as a base; but Port Royal in Jamaica and, to a lesser extent, New Providence in the Bahamas provided facilities as well.

Some enterprising men attempted to form new settlements along the mainland shores of the Caribbean, ostensibly to wage what would amount to private wars against the Spaniards, and, believe it or not, 'against pirates'. In one of his books about the West Indies[3] written at the time the Duke of Albemarle was Governor of Jamaica, Sir Hans Sloane describes how the Duke was visited by various characters from the settlements. Their request was to obtain official recognition of the settlements and powers to conduct hostilities. The Duke rightly considered that any such recognition would be tantamount to endorsing what would merely become government by pirates for pirates.

It must not be supposed that every European then in the West Indies was dishonest; there was plenty of money to be made by growing sugar cane, which had become the staple commercial crop after its introduction from the Canary Islands in the previous century. The demand in Europe for sugar increased rapidly, and planters of all nationalities tried to create settlements and plantations in many uninhabited islands admirably suitable for this purpose. But the Spaniards would have none of this in a part of the world over which they claimed complete domination. The result was that many a peaceful planter ultimately joined the cause against a common enemy. Once on the downward path . . .

Notes

1. *Histoire de l'isle de St. Dominque.* P. F. X. Charlevoic. Paris, 1730.
2. *Carte Résduit de l'isle de St. Domingo.*
3. *Natural History of Jamaica,* Vol. 1, 76.

CHAPTER XIII

THE SEQUEL TO TORTUGA

THE STRIKING SUCCESSES of the buccaneers in the Caribbean gradually made good prizes at sea increasingly difficult to find, so thought was given to the practicability of attacks on rich Spanish coastal cities in the New World, to obtain treasure at source rather than in transit to Europe. Such attacks resembled those made much earlier by Elizabethan and other seamen from Europe. That locally-organised attacks were possible was first demonstrated by Henry Morgan at Campeachy in 1665, and, five years later, by his successful attack on Panama. From his base at Port Royal, Jamaica, Morgan was able to muster as many as 1,400 men locally for this venture with the assistance given by the governor of Jamaica.

Morgan's successes prompted others to have a go. In 1683 van Horn, a Dutchman, collected six buccaneer ships from Hispaniola for an attack on Vera Cruz in Mexico. For the expedition he was assisted by three experienced French pirates, Laurence de Graff, Godfrey, and Jonque, with whom he had been associated for a long time. Van Horn was renowned for the way in which under no circumstances would he permit the slightest sign of hesitation or cowardice among those he led, and in an engagement he walked about his ship closly observing everything that happened. If anyone shrank or started at a pistol or gunshot he killed him immediately, a form of discipline which endeared him to the brave, but made him a holy terror to anyone at all faint-hearted. Until the Vera Cruz attack van Horn invariably sailed alone in his own ship, his personal property, but he was always scrupulously fair in the division of the vast treasures captured.

One thousand two hundred men, mostly French, were recruited for this successful and profitable mainland raid in which £437,500 was obtained in loot and ransom money. The raiders landed in darkness nine miles from Vera Cruz which they reached without being discovered. The whole place was taken and occupied by daylight, a great triumph over professional soldiers by men who were really undisciplined seamen. Then all the citizens were shut up in the churches without anything to eat or drink for three days, with barrels of gunpowder in position to blow up any groups who were slow in coming to terms for their ransom. The getaway was equally bold. As they were about to withdraw a Spanish fleet of 17 ships arrived from Europe. When these ships were sighted the raiders hastily collected their loot, including 1,500 slaves as a bit of makeweight, and set sail, bearing straight through the Spanish vessels which did not even open fire. This forbearance was thought to be due to the risk of provoking an attack by Van Horn's ships with likely consequences. The buccaneers themselves were not really interested in the arrivals from Europe, which would only be loaded with ordinary merchandise of little use to them, when they already had plenty of loot.

This success had far-reaching results and greatly influenced the subsequent code of pirate practice in the New World. The attack demonstrated that untrained but ruthless men could, if well led, match up to Spanish armed forces, and that Spanish riches could be tapped at source and not necessarily on the high seas. The year after the raid on Vera Cruz both the English and the French decided quite independently to arrange attacks on Peru, the country from which came most of the South American treasure. The English were led by men named David Samins, Peter Milmer and Townley. Had there been proper liaison between the various raiders on Peru it is quite likely that this country might have been wrested from the Spaniards, more particularly if the raiders had received help from their home governments.

Peru had already been colonised for over a century, and there were many well-established towns and cities along its Pacific seaboard. Apart from precious metals and jewels it was the country from which also originated things such as cloth, sweetmeats, and flour from the wheat first introduced into the Americas by the Spaniards. The difficulty was to get there; either this involved a voyage around South America, which was the route favoured by the French, or else the difficult journey overland, somewhere south of Panama, after which ships had to be captured for use along the Pacific coast. Men travelling by either route had prearranged meeting-places. Judged by any standards the overland crossing of the Darien Isthmus was itself a remarkable achievement, although in later years it was a journey made quite frequently by parties of marauders going to and from the Pacific. The fastest passage by any European at Panama was three days, but an Indian could make it in 36 hours. A first-hand account of one journey from the Pacific side later in the 17th century was written by Lionel Wafer, the surgeon.[1] Like many others he suffered severe privations and vicissitudes, but survived to return to England where he settled down in practice.

This extract from *The Daily Telegraph* in 1971, over 300 years later, is revealing:

> A British team is to attempt the first vehicle crossing of the 250 mile Isthmus of Darien, which joins Panama to Colombia. It links North and South America. The isthmus has been crossed on foot, but previous attempts on wheels ended with the loss of vehicles in the swamp. Snakes, mosquitos, dense jungle, ravines, swamps, heat and skin diseases make it among the most difficult terrain in the world. It is the last remaining section of the Pan-American Highway linking the Americas still to be completed.

Once the Pacific was reached, ships there, including naval vessels, fell victims to their poorly-equipped but determined opponents; after obtaining local command of the sea, these men raided Peru at will despite interruptions by several squadrons sent to oppose them. Such interruptions, however, meant that many pirate ships were longer at sea than anticipated, and often experienced serious food shortages which could only be relieved by shore raids simply to obtain urgently-needed supplies. Still, the raids to get booty were highly successful and few towns escaped a visit. It is quite surprising that there was not more opposition by the garrisons possessed by most places; many towns were deserted by the inhabitants directly the enemy was sighted, since the pirates rarely gave much quarter.

As soon as a town was occupied it was burnt unless a sum calculated from its size was paid over as a ransom. Any prisoners taken were immediately massacred if not ransomed by the local governor or some of the inhabitants. The only ransoms acceptable were in gold, pearls or precious stones. Silver was too common and too unwieldy in quantity to be of any interest. It was remarked at the time that during these raids the Spaniards paid in full for their cruelties to the Incas when they first invaded Peru.

From then onwards raids on to the Pacific coast towns became quite frequent; some started from across the Darien Isthmus, while others were by ships which made the long voyage from Europe via Cape Horn. Perhaps the most noteworthy of these was made by *Cygnet,* under Captain Swan, who was financed by some London merchants of all people. It was in this ship that the celebrated William Dampier served as quartermaster; Basil Ringrose, gentleman adventurer, was the navigator, and Lionel Wafer the surgeon.

The well-known book by Esquemeling, the Dutchman, mainly describes activities around Terra Firma, Darien and the Pacific. This book had a large circulation, but has been shown to be inaccurate in various respects, despite the fact that it actually incorporates much material provided by Basil Ringrose who was killed in 1686.

Meanwhile in the North Sea, as the Caribbean Sea used to be called, piracy was carried on by various lone wolves, though in the course of time several big shore raids were undertaken as combined operations. As the home government began to take more interest in French Hispaniola governors were appointed from Paris. To begin with governors had to accept piracy as the most important local industry, but gradually they tried to induce the men involved to become planters, and some progress was finally achieved. This was all upset shortly after the arrival of a man named Gramont. Gramont was a former French army officer who had distinguished himself in Europe; but wine, women, and song led to his downfall, and he had emigrated and become a pirate. His attributes, such as a cultured background, a pleasing personality and sound judgement soon led him to be regarded as the chief of the French buccaneers, and the local men were anxious to come under his command. In 1685, with such support as was available, he decided to attack the prosperous city of Campeachy himself. Through this place, as in Morgan's time, passed much of the valuable produce of Central America, particularly timber and the logwood in demand for dyeing. Initially, Gramont discussed his project with the French governor who forbade it in the king's name, to which Gramont replied, 'How can Louis [XIV] disapprove of a design he is unacquainted with and only planned a few days ago'.

The raid duly took place and the landing was without opposition, but later they were attacked by 800 Spaniards whom they drove into the city. There in street fighting the buccaneers prevailed; only the citadel held out, but not for long. Strange to say the master gunner of the citadel was an Englishman who had shown such courage that Gramont received him personally, and, after giving him some presents, released him. The buccaneers spent two months in and around the place collecting everything portable of value, and then entered into negotiations with the Spanish governor about the fate of the city itself: if it were not ransomed it would be burned. Before these negotiations were completed came the festival of St. Louis, the royal anniversary, and in a drunken spree a million pounds' worth of logwood was burned. Without more ado they all returned home.

Ultimately gangs of all nationalities operated from local bases established in suitable islands off the Pacific coast of the New World and in the Caribbean. The bases of choice in the Caribbean were mainly in the northern end of the Leeward Islands, which lay in a good strategic position for attacking the most popular shipping lanes in and around the Windward Passage, which the gangs knew so well. Local knowledge by robbers anywhere always helps their activities, and such knowledge often gave pirates an advantage in many parts of the world. Their use by pirates serves to explain the diverse European background of certain West Indian islands even today. The Danish Virgin Islands were actually purchased by the U.S.A. this century. The only European nation not to retain permanent footholds in the Caribbean were the Swedes, but many Swedes participated in those lucrative attacks.

It is clear that the buccaneer period, lasting nearly a century, was characterised by the loosely-working local partnership mainly between the French and the English, with help from men of other European nationalities. The mix-up in Central America was curious. In Europe their homelands might be at war, but, overseas, men from any country would happily serve at sea alongside each other. Most of this liaison came to an end after the repeated wars between the English and the French home governments, beginning about 1700 and lasting until Waterloo in 1815.

Notes

1. *A New Voyage and Descriptions of the Isthmus of America.* 1699.
2. *The Colonising Activities of the English Puritans.* L. Newton. Yale University Press, 1914.

CHAPTER XIV

SOME NOTABLES

A NUMBER of biographical sketches have been written about various men whose achievements have aroused special interest. Most of these sketches portray a fairly constant and somewhat sordid pattern of life: of men who often started as competent mariners, but who were tempted and, occasionally, after being taken prisoner forced to adopt a way of life which usually ended on the gallows.

However, there were some whose lives perhaps were sordid, but in whom greed was not the sole motive for their activities. There were those whose sheer achievements, regardless of the underlying motive, must arouse admiration by almost anyone. What certain men did can only make one wonder what they might have accomplished if their talents had been applied in a more orthodox fashion. Or, would they have ever found themselves in a position, perhaps in the Fighting Services, to use their abilities to the full? Further, if in the Services, would the existing systems of patronage and promotion ever have given them much chance to obtain command?

Take the case of John Plantan, born in Jamaica in about 1700, who went to sea as a boy of 13, an age quite usual in those days. While in his late teens he got into bad company with other youths, some of whom were already almost fully-fledged pirates. Plantan was persuaded to become one himself and before long he quitted the Atlantic seaboard for Madagascar, where his powers of leadership were soon recognised. While still in his early twenties, and already highly successful, he became involved in the politics of the pirate republics in Madagascar. And his involvement was not simply as a conventional politician, but as a military commander of repute. With headquarters at Port Dauphin, where he was dictator, he undertook various campaigns against other parts of the island, using Malagasy troops mostly armed in European style. After numerous successes he practically became king of the whole island, and a powerful king at that. However, it was inevitable that he had personal enemies, mostly due to jealousy, and he realised he could not hold his position indefinitely; so, after a year or two, he decided to get out while the going was good. He had already married a local woman with whom he was very much in love, and the couple left Madagascar for India. There, it is to be hoped, they settled down and lived happily ever after; but nothing is known of his later life. John Avery, mentioned on page 117, who attained renown some 25 years earlier in the same part of the world, is still often mentioned for his prowess, but this was nothing like so outstanding as the diversity of Plantan's activities.

In the early days of piracy in and around the Spanish Main and the Caribbean from the time of Drake onwards, most, if not all, English seamen conducted their operations from Europe; only later did they base operations locally. After the first French colonists in the West Indies suffered so severely from the Spaniards, a number of the Frenchmen who had lost relatives in the West Indies, or felt strongly about Spanish behaviour, left France to help the English and Dutch conduct what were to all intents and purposes private, and often profitable, wars in the New World. One gently-born Frenchman, named De Mont, left France to become leader of a gang simply to avenge the death of relatives among the early colonists. Another Frenchman, Montbar from Languedoc, will always be remembered because of the unusual circumstances affecting his career. As a boy he heard about the cruelties of the Spaniards to the Indians, something which developed in him a frenzy against a nation which could act in such a fashion. To try and avenge this wrong he decided when he was old enough to go to the Caribbean and join the buccaneers, of whom he had heard and who were known to be the inveterate enemies of Spain. His adventures began during the voyage to the New World when a Spanish vessel was encountered and, as was usual at the time, attacked and boarded. Montbar, sabre in hand, was foremost in a successful engagement, and it was reported how twice he went from end to end of the ship felling every Spaniard within reach. After their surrender there was a rich booty to divide, but Montbar contented himself with the pleasure of contemplating the heaps of bodies of those against whom for so long he had felt such hatred. Little wonder that, later on, he became known as The Exterminator.

At a later period the Frenchman L'Ollonais took the plunge under quite different circumstances. He was one of many Europeans who emigrated to the West Indies to benefit from the increasing prosperity of these island colonies. Once there, unless a young man had local family connections or influence, the only way he could get on his feet was to become a bondman to one of the established planters or traders. Ostensibly this bondmanship resembled an apprenticeship, but in practice, particularly if the masters were unscrupulous, it was a life little better than slavery. Many disillusioned youths tried to escape; the escape routes were few, yet once aboard a pirate vessel they were safe from irate masters. L'Ollonais made his escape from a French island with two canoes and 22 men. With this small force he captured a Spanish frigate off the coast of Cuba, and so started a successful new life which included an attack on Maracaibo in 1666.

Dampier, the famous navigator born in Somerset, after serving his apprenticeship, subsequently went to Java in an East Indiaman to improve his navigation; later he served for a year in a British warship, *Royal Prince,* during the Dutch war of 1673. At the end of this time he accepted an offer to manage a plantation in Jamaica, but shipped as a seaman to avoid the risk to passengers if the ship were captured on the way. On his arrival in Jamaica he soon discovered that plantation life was not for him, so he served in ships engaged in the local and quite legitimate mahogany and logwood trade around the Bay of Campeachy. Due to various adverse circumstances, mainly as the result of a severe storm, he found himself impoverished on the beach. Fortunately for him a privateer (so often an euphemism for a pirate ship) came to where he was; this he gladly joined, and his knowledge of seamanship and navigation was welcomed. So began the more adventurous period of his life, and some years elapsed before he resumed a more orthodox existence, culminating in his voyage round the world. This is graphically described in the books he wrote afterwards.

One colourful character often mentioned is Dr. Blood, said to have been practising in Bridgwater at the time of the nearby battle of Sedgemoor in 1685 which ended the Monmouth rebellion. He was called to treat one of his regular patients who had been wounded in the battle. Some of Colonel Kirke's troopers, searching for rebels, found him carrying out his ordinary professional duties. Because the doctor was treating a rebel he was deemed to be one himself, and was arrested together with a master mariner named Pitt, who was an unwounded refugee from the battle. After trial at Taunton by Judge Jeffreys both men were sentenced to death, but were later reprieved and deported to the West Indies to become slaves on the plantations. The story of Dr. Blood is told in an historical novel by Sabatini entitled the *Saga of the Sea,* in which the author clearly cites documentary evidence for his tale; this tale, needless to say, is of much interest in Bridgwater. It has proved impossible to trace the documentary basis for the story despite searches by various people. I myself have examined the original list of prisoners reprieved after the Taunton Bloody Assize, but this does not help. Many highly respectable Somerset men, including peers, churchmen, and country gentlemen, who supported Monmouth and who were sentenced to transportation, were sold in Barbados as slaves to the planters, some for 1,500lbs. of sugar each. A few of these escaped and became pirates, together with other Europeans who for one reason or another found themselves in bondage.

A well-known story concerns Henry Pitman, a surgeon who happened to be in Taunton the day after the fighting on Sedgemoor. Out of sheer humanity he treated wounded from both armies, otherwise completely neglected and lying about in the town; yet, because he had treated wounded rebels, Pitman was arrested and later sold into slavery in Barbados. After despicable treatment for over a year in this island he escaped with five other Monmouth men to Tortuga, that important pirate base, where they were welcomed. Pitman, however, refused to join up with them, and after further adventures finally reached England, where, during his absence, he had been pardoned. The other men who had escaped with him from Barbados seized a small pirate ship in which they started to sail to New England; but on their way they were captured, strangely enough, by another pirate ship. Finally they were released in Jamaica, whence they made their way back to England. It is just possible that the story of Dr. Blood may be a writer's imaginative reconstruction of the experiences of Henry Pitman.

Although Sabatini states that Blood successfully attacked Maracaibo (Venezuela) after becoming a pirate chief, the only authentic records of successful attacks on that important Spanish city were by L'Ollonais, already mentioned, in 1666, and another by Henry Morgan in 1670. However, it is known that various gangs 'had a go' at Maracaibo, but details about these attacks are lacking. For his attack on Maracaibo L'Ollonais was in partnership with another buccaneer named Michael de Basco, who had distinguished himself, among other successes, by capturing a Spanish ship with treasure estimated to be worth no less than £218,500, the equivalent of several million pounds sterling today. Such were the prizes to be got. The Maracaibo attack by L'Ollonais and de Basco could have been even more rewarding than it proved to be had not a couple of weeks been wasted in a drinking debauch in Gibraltar, the town at the entrance to Lake Maracaibo, after the entire garrison of 250 men had been put to death. By the time Maracaibo was reached much of its treasure had been removed and hidden, but, nevertheless, a big haul of valuables and ransom money was made. Among the valuables taken were many church ornaments and even the bells, all of which, it was announced at the time, were to be used in a new chapel to be built in Tortuga. It was a remarkable idea that loot of this nature should be put to such a purpose.

It has already been shown how busy the French were in the Caribbean in the 17th century, with some of their organised raids being undertaken from Europe in much the same way as the English had been doing during the previous century. The attack by de Pontis and Du Casse on Cartagena in 1697, the last of its kind ever made, produced one of the biggest single hauls in history. The main expedition sailed from France, while Du Casse, the governor of the French part of Hispaniola, recruited over a thousand local toughs to strengthen the force under de Pontis. After an initial bombardment the combined force stormed strongpoint after strongpoint until the city surrendered, when the inhabitants were guaranteed protection by de Pontis. But the combined landing parties of French regulars and pirates could not be held, and drink and lust took charge. An appalling situation lasted for two days until order was restored by fresh troops and seamen from ships lying off-shore. One and three quarter million pounds of valuables were seized, that is to say, something approaching twenty million pounds at today's value.

By an earlier agreement, 1,200,000 louis (a gold coin first struck in France in 1640, then worth about 0.80p) were to be distributed among the locally-recruited pirates for their help. However, de Pontis sailed for home before this was paid out. His own men also began to enquire about a share of the loot; they must already have learnt from the locals something about the customary way this was done. De Pontis then tried to double cross the men, rather like Morgan had done some 20 years earlier after his profitable attack on Panama. He offered £5,250 for his men's share (how this odd sum was arrived at is not clear) and, needless to say, it was turned down flat. Some of the aggrieved men wished to board de Pontis's ship, *Sceptre,* and deal with him there and then. Wiser councils prevailed, and a number of ships were seized by the defrauded men and sailed back to Cartagena, where a fresh onslaught was made. It was entered without any resistance; what had become of the original

Spanish garrison is not known. Immediately all the men in the city were shut up in a large church, and a demand was made by the raiders for £218,750, considered to be the money to which they were entitled. They undertook to leave directly they had received this, but threatened the worst if they were not paid. A venerable priest entered the pulpit and persuaded his audience to deliver up all their valuables, many of which must have been hidden during the earlier attack. The value of the collection made as a result of the priest's efforts did not reach the required sum, so the city was plundered again. After some delay the invading ships finally left. Several were taken or sunk by Spanish naval vessels in the open sea, but the others escaped to Tortuga and Haiti.

Another interesting character was named Greaves. He was born in Barbados to English parents originally sent by Cromwell to that island as slaves. Transported with his parents were other prisoners, mostly Scots or Irish, who, for some reason or other, were locally known as Red Legs. Young Greaves managed to escape, and joined a ship commanded by a Captain Hawkins, who was notoriously cruel. Because he did not approve of unnecessary bloodshed and the torture and killing of non-combatants, Greaves finally quarrelled with his captain with whom he fought a duel. He won this duel, assumed command himself, and was very successful, finally retiring to become a West Indian planter. One well-educated Frenchman named Raveneau de Lussau had to flee from his homeland in debt, but in the Caribbean he was fortunate in making a packet. In due course he actually married a wealthy Spanish widow, and the couple settled down on the west coast of South America. Few were ever able to achieve anything like this; they met their end too soon.

Long after Greaves's time, during the reign of Queen Anne, there was an Englishman in Barbados named Major Bonnet. He had served during the War of the Spanish Succession (the war in which Sir Winston Churchill's ancestor, the Duke of Marlborough so distinguished himself). At the end of the war in 1713, after the Treaty of Utrecht, Bonnet found himself without occupation. Although he knew nothing much about the sea he decided to go into business as a pirate. To do so he acquired a suitable ship, engaged a captain and somehow obtained a sufficiently bloodthirsty crew. There were inevitable frictions in this strange combination, and the enterprise was particularly hazardous, as ever since 1689 pirates had been outlawed. Somehow or other the venture survived for two years, but the inevitable end came and Bonnet was hanged in Charleston, South Carolina, in 1718 (Plate 12).

Bartholomew Roberts is still remembered for his dubious but remarkable career in the early 18th century, during which he is said to have captured about 400 ships. A man named Edward England, associated with him, was probably even more outstanding. As a dyed-in-the-wool pirate he demonstrated in the Indian Ocean that an Englishman was able to show courage and resourcefulness, misapplied perhaps, as good as that of the Frenchman Surcouf, whose activities in that ocean later in the century are so often mentioned. England was originally mate of a Jamaican merchantman captured by pirates and, probably because he had no option, he became one himself. He soon obtained a command, and when American waters became too hot he chose the West African coast as a new sphere of operations, where he was remarkably successful. The chief victims were English merchantmen on the triangular run—euphemistically called the West Indian sugar trade—from England to the Guinea Coast, with a general cargo of which part was discharged in West Africa and the remainder in the West Indies.

What is not always appreciated was the small size of so many of the ships trading regularly in the Atlantic: they were mostly of 50–80 tons, and some even smaller. Of the seven England captured in just one month, May 1718, only one had a crew exceeding 18 hands, and that was *Brentworth* of Bristol with a crew of thirty. It was another Bristol ship, *Peterborough,* subsequently renamed *Victory,* in which England later voyaged to the Indian Ocean from West Africa in company with a Dutch prize. Before quitting the Atlantic there was one of those frequent gang quarrels, and a number of dissidents ranged themselves under Bartholomew Roberts, who sailed away with his party to carve out his own career in one of the many prize ships available.

There is uncertainty about the extent of England's first cruise, but he is known to have selected the island of Johanna (between Madagascar and Mozambique) as his operational base. This was the island used 26 years earlier by John Avery, as already mentioned. Johanna was one of the places favoured by East Indiamen for a respite on their long voyages. On returning to this island in *Fancy* and *Victory* after a successful foray to the Red Sea, England found two ships of the British East India Company lying in a bay together with a ship from the Austrian Netherlands. One of the company's ships, *Cassandra*, was commanded by Captain Mackray, in his day the most renowned of the East Indiamen masters. He was shamefully deserted by the other two ships and left to fight it out with England. Then began what was nothing short of a naval engagement between the East Indiaman and the two pirate ships, a battle lasting about three hours. Finally *Cassandra* was boarded in customary fashion. Captain Mackray, although wounded in the head, managed to escape ashore with some survivors from his ship. This boarding of *Cassandra* demonstrates again the unpalatable fact that once pirates gained a proper foothold on the deck of any merchantman the ship was theirs. In this instance success against an East Indiaman was possible because England caught her at a disadvantage.

After about ten days ashore, with the knowledge that he and his companions might well become marooned, Captain Mackray boldly went and sought an interview with England: after all, Mackray was a well-known shipmaster. The outcome of what must have been a tricky interview was that England allowed Mackray to take over *Fancy*, seriously damaged in the fight. In this he was permitted to make his way to Bombay as best he could, a voyage he made with the survivors from *Cassandra*, jury-rigged, in 48 days. England came off well, because *Cassandra*, with her cargo and £75,000 in cash on board, now became a pirate ship to sail in consort with *Victory*.

Despite special endeavours by the East India Company to catch them, these two ships literally ran amuck all over the Indian Ocean, taking prizes at will. On one occasion in the Mascarines they excelled themselves by capturing a Portuguese ship of 70 guns while lying at anchor to repair gale damage. On board was the Viceroy of Goa who was released on ransom for 2,000 dollars, a small sum compared with the vast loot from the ship. She was carrying a quantity of diamonds, apart from other treasures, and each pirate received 42 diamonds over and above his ordinary share of the spoils.

After this episode, the Royal Navy tried to catch England, who, possibly more by luck than good management, still evaded capture. But England and many of his men must have felt that they had been so successful that they had better not push their luck any further. So stop they did and spread themselves among the pirate republics of Madagascar, where England died, somewhat unusually for a pirate, in bed. Apparently towards his end he became very penitent for his misdeeds.

Robert Surcouf (1773–1827) can be regarded as the last of the freebooters, and what a career he had! Until the end of the Napoleonic wars France had many possessions and footholds in the Indian Ocean, where trading was very active in every way. Surcouf was a Frenchman originally in the slave trade. After the French Revolution, when the Convention declared the slave trade illegal, he and others simply carried on as before in those waters far from France, amassing fortunes. When the limited strength of the British blockade in the Indian Ocean was realised by the governor of Bourbon (Réunion) he mustered two French frigates and two privateers which successfully raised the blockade on Bourbon and Mauritius. Thereafter, and for a long time, French ships could come and go at will, so Surcouf resumed his slave trading. Somehow he got at loggerheads with the local French authorities, and when he decided he was sufficiently wealthy to turn privateer, to his dismay he was refused the necessary Letter of Marque by the governor of Bourbon. Nothing daunted, he decided to go pirating. His slaving ship was quite unsuitable for this, but he managed to obtain a rather better one, *Emile,* of 180 tons, ostensibly to trade between the French islands. Like any other merchantman the ship was armed for defence purposes, but only with four six-pounders. After adding to his crew at the Seychelles he renounced any pretences at trading and operated as a pirate around the Andamans and Sumatra, where he obtained his first prize. Soon afterwards he captured a Dutch East Indiaman homeward bound with £15,000 of gold on board, together with a valuable cargo of rice, pepper and sugar; this was easily sold in Mauritius, where there was always a chronic food shortage. Then Surcouf sailed to the approaches of Calcutta, soon to take three merchantmen and an escort pilot brig. This latter ship was much better suited to his purpose, so he commissioned her for himself and named her *Cartier.* Despite the need to put prize crews on board his captures it seems he was able to find the fresh hands needed because men of various nationalities were anxious to profit by association with someone so famous.

The one-time Calcutta pilot brig was for a while able to operate off the Orissa coast without arousing suspicion until her new role was revealed to victims. That was how *Cartier* was able to take *Triton* by surprise with a boarding party of only 19 men. *Triton* was one of the finest East Indiamen of her time, mounting 26 guns; she had even been used as an armed merchant cruiser to protect British shipping in the China Sea. Admittedly she was at anchor when attacked, and very pertinent questions were asked after the event about the absence of any proper look-out or preparedness for a possible attack in a region where hostile craft were known to be operating. That such things could happen anywhere was once demonstrated in the Straits of Dover when a large British East Indiaman, homeward-bound, was taken by the French because she could not use her guns in time due to their being cluttered up with passengers' luggage. Even after demonstrating his undoubted skill as a fighting seaman Surcouf was unable to make the French Administration in the Indian Ocean regard him as anything better than a common pirate. So, at his own expense, he travelled to Paris where he was finally granted a Letter of Marque to become a privateer. His later career in a fine Nantes ship, which he took back to the Indian Ocean, was even more successful than his previous exploits in that Ocean when he was operating simply for his own personal profit.

Once British sea power became fully established all over the world after the Napoleonic Wars, Surcouf and others like him did not have a chance, and the days of common piracy were numbered.

APPENDIX I

Reading a story in which evil seems to triumph, we derive a particular satisfaction when, at the end, the villain gets his just deserts. Sir Ralph was such a villain, and *The Inchcape Rock* brings him to the end he deserves.

The Inchcape Rock

No stir in the air, no stir in the sea—
The ship was as still as she could be;
Her sails from heaven received no motion;
Her keel was steady in the ocean.

Without either sign or sound of their shock,
The waves flowed over the Inchcape rock;
So little they rose, so little they fell,
They did not move the Inchcape bell.

The holy Abbot of Aberbrothok
Had placed that bell on the Inchcape rock;
On a buoy in the storm it floated and swung
And over the waves it warning rung.

When the rock was hid by the surges swell,
The mariners heard the warning bell;
And then they knew the perilous rock,
And blessed the Abbot of Aberbrothok.

The sun in heaven was shining gay—
All things were joyful on that day;
The sea-birds screamed as they wheeled around,
And there was joyance in their sound.

The buoy of the Inchcape bell was seen,
A darker speck on the ocean green;
Sir Ralph, the rover, walked his deck,
And he fixed his eyes on the darker speck.

His eye was on the bell and float;
Quoth he, 'My men, put out the boat:
And row me to the Inchcape rock,
And I'll plague the priest of Aberbrothok'.

The boat is lowered, the boatmen row,
And to the Inchcape rock they go;
Sir Ralph bent over the boat,
And cut the warning bell from the float.

Down sank the bell with a gurgling sound;
The bubbles rose, and burst around.
Quoth Sir Ralph, 'The next who comes to the rock
Will not bless the Abbot of Aberbrothok'.

Sir Ralph, the rover, sailed away—
He scoured the seas for many a day;
And now, grown rich with plundered store,
He steers the course to Scotland's shore.

So thick a haze o'erspreads the sky
They cannot see the sun on high;
The wind hath blown a gale all day;
At evening it hath died away.

On the deck the rover takes his stand;
So dark it is they see no land.
Quoth Sir Ralph, 'It will be lighter soon,
For there is the dawn of the rising moon'.

'Canst hear', said one, 'the breakers roar?
For yonder, methinks, should be the shore.
Now where we are I cannot tell,
But I wish we could hear the Inchcape bell'.

They hear no sound; the swell is strong;
Though the wind hath fallen, they drift along;
Till the vessel strikes with a shivering shock—
O Christ! it is the Inchcape rock!

Sir Ralph, the rover, tore his hair;
He cursed himself in his despair.
The waves rush in on every side;
The ship is sinking beneath the tide.

But ever in his dying fear
One dreadful sound he seemed to hear—
A sound as if with the Inchcape bell
The Devil below was ringing his knell.

Robert Southey

APPENDIX II

Further Reading (Selective List)

A Relation of the great Sufferings and Strange Adventures of Henry Pitman. An English Garner. Arber. 1877.

The Voyages and Adventures of Captain William Dampier. Various volumes.

Doctrines of Naval Architecture. Deane, 1675.

Les pirates à Madagascar au XVIIme et XVIIIme siècles. Des Champs. 1949.

Buccaneers of America. Esquemeling. Various editions.

The Madagascar Pirates. Forster. 1957.

Hydrographie. Fournier. 1667.

Elizabethan Seamen. Froude. 1910.

The Pirates Who's Who. Gosse. 1923.

Quina-quina. Haggis, G. Bull. Hist. Med. 10, 417.

A General History of the Robbers, Murderers, and most notorious Pirates. (17th century.) Johnson, Hayward ed. 1926.

Stuart Tracts. Constable. 1903.

Journal du Voyage fait à la Mer de Sud avec Les Filibustiers de l'Amerique en 1684.

The Modern Traveller. Various volumes. 1790–1810.

Monograph on Chinese Maritime Affairs. Encl. Britt, 1st Edn.

Flacourt. Paris, 1660. *Hist. de la Grand Isle de Madagascar.*

Many other references will be found in the text.

GENERAL INDEX

Algiers, 64
Antarctic, 106
Arabs, 36
Arabia, 44
Archers, 17
Attacks, 107-8
Auto da Fé, 76
Azores, 20

Bahamas, 41, 123, 141
Baltic, 25, 63
Banking, 72
Barbados, 10, 153-4
Barbary Coast, 3
Beys, 4, 91
Biblical refs., 13, 19
Bias Bay, 54
Blood groups, 20
Boarding, 100
Bodies, 33
Bonds, 8
Borneo, 52
Bourbon, 71,
Bristol, 22, 30-1, 42, 65, 79, 81, 127
British Isles, 14, 16
Broadhaven, 27-8
Brotherhood, 83
Bucan, 4
Buccaneers, 133
Byblos, 13

Campeachy, 69, 148
Canals, 16, 18
Canary Isles, 20
Cannibals, 4, 10
Cannon, 48, 101-2, 160
Caribs, 132
Cartagena, 95, 155
Cape Verde Isles, 128-9
Careening, 136
Carpentry, 106, 111
Cayona, 135, 137
Central Africa, 19

Charlestown, 86
Charter Companies, 11, 14, 39, 45-6, 50, 59, 78, 135
Charters, 10
China, 46-7, 50
Cinque Ports, 28
Compensation, 116
Convoys, 10
Cooking, 109
Copper trade, 18
Corsairs, 3, 22, 28, 63
Crab Island, 40
Crete, 12, 18
Cutlass, 105, 141

Darien, 112, 146-7
Defences, 10, 27
Definitions, 2
Dunkirk, 8
Divine Service, 33, 116
Dover, 34
Drinks, 109
Dutch, 3, 28, 35, 133
Dyes, 60-1

East Indiamen, 11
Egyptians, 13
English law, 2, 8-9
Ezion-Geber, 17-18

Far East, 14
Fishermen, 32, 74
Flags, 117-9
Flintlocks, 105, 141
Fore & aft rig, 35
Freebooter, 5

Gaming houses, 93
Garb, 111-2
Glasses, 118
Greenwich Hospital, 9
Greeks, 14
Guinea Coast, 10, 40, 96, 120, 137, 15

INDEX OF PEOPLE

INDEX OF SHIPS